REPRESENT

THE WOMAN'S GUIDE TO RUNNING FOR OFFICE & CHANGING THE WORLD

JUNE DIANE RAPHAEL
and KATE BLACK

Workman Publishing ★ New York

Library of Congress Cataloging-in-Publication Data is available.

ISBN 978-1-5235-0297-4

Design by Becky Terhune
Illustrations by Noli Novak
Author photos by Jessica Caso (Kate Black) and courtesy of Netflix (June Diane Raphael)

Workman books are available at special discounts when purchased in bulk for premiums and sales promotions as well as for fund-raising or educational use. Special editions or book excerpts can also be created to specification. For details, contact the Special Sales Director at the address below, or send an email to specialmarkets@workman.com.

Workman Publishing Co., Inc.
225 Varick Street
New York, NY 10014-4381
workman.com

Printed in China
First printing August 2019

10 9 8 7 6 5 4 3 2 1

We dedicate this book to all the men who have been
making decisions about women . . . without women.
Thank you for your years of public service at tables
without women present. Thank you for your time,
your energy, and your talent. We appreciate you.

And also . . . *we're coming for you.*

Contents

A Letter from
JUNE AND KATE

JUNE

Dear Reader,

On election night, November 8, 2016, I (June Diane Raphael, actress-writer-podcaster–hyphenate haver) boarded a red-eye from LA to NY to go to a funeral, which would turn out to be one of the brighter spots of the next few days. The two other seats in my row were empty. A news notification popped up on my phone as I settled into my seat. The state of Florida was called for Trump. Alone in my row, I was feeling—how to put this—shaky.

At takeoff I still thought there was a way for this to turn around. There just had to be. But when we reached our cruising altitude, CNN correspondent John King was on the television explaining there was no path for Hillary. I stared at him. I wondered what happened with him and Dana Bash and why they didn't go the distance. And then I wondered if this was real life and if Hillary had actually lost or if the plane had crashed and I was a ghost? Being a ghost didn't seem all that—

A man scooted up from his full row behind me and sat in the aisle seat of my row. He had seen an open seat and, well . . . he was gonna take it. He started taking out his computer and setting himself up.

Nope. Nah. No fucking way, dude.

"Sir, I'm so sorry. I actually bought all of the seats in this row. That's mine. That seat is mine."

Because we are just meeting, Dear Reader, please know that I'm not usually in the business of lying to strangers. But when this very sweet man looked up at me, I saw something in his eyes. A hint of recognition? Maybe he knew me from TV? The Netflix series *Grace and Frankie?* From my podcast *How Did This Get Made?* From a guest-star role I did on the failed NBC sitcom *Animal Practice*, in which I played opposite a monkey? I tried to make my face somehow look more recognizable—a strange endeavor. But somehow, some way, this man nodded, saying, "Of course," and started to pack up his things.

Of course!

Of course, I had purchased AN ENTIRE ROW, like any other actress of mild fame would! The truth was I simply could not bear to be with anyone as election night unfolded. I needed those seats. Not for my body; I needed them for my damn mind.

I won't take you through the rest of the flight. I'll only mention that when the 270 electoral votes came in, a very intoxicated man in first class jumped up screaming with joy and then started gyrating against his seat. Quick, purposeful thrusts were accompanied by lots of "OH YEAHs." Hillary had lost. Donald Trump had won. And I was watching a man hump a seat.

My eyes popped open the next morning. I sat up from the empty row I had not purchased, defensively pulled my coat over my Hillary T-shirt, and peered down the aisle to see where the chair rapist was. To make matters so much worse, he was cozied up in a blanket snug as a bug in a rug, sleeping peacefully in the very seat he'd had his way with just hours before. And I thought . . .

Should I run for office?

But seriously, I thought to myself, *should I? If Trump is qualified to be our president, am I not just as qualified? Maybe even more so?* I stared at my row. Were there more seats to claim as my own? Without explanation or apology?

But where would I begin? What would I run for? What about my past? I've for sure texted topless pics to various gentlemen callers in my day. Does that disqualify me altogether? What would I do about my career? My children? I already feel like I don't spend enough time with them. How much money would I need to raise? And . . . what about those pics again?

I had no idea how to answer these questions. I searched for a current, comprehensive guide and came up empty-handed. But it turns out there was a woman who could answer all of my questions. Here's how I found her.

Remembering that my friend Morgan mentioned she'd gone to a fundraiser for EMILY's List (an organization dedicated to getting pro-choice Democratic women into office), I sent her the following text:

Ignore the last part of that text exchange, thanks.

Hi! Do U have a contact at Emily's list? I want to get some information or resources on why women run, don't run, challenges they face etc.

Yes! I'll send to u

Thank u!

My friend got back to me she's been in Mexico and back to work tmrw! (Emily's list)

Thank U! Getting my first period back after a year and Morgan . . . I feel insane. I literally am a hormonal werewolf!

I'm introduced to a woman named Michelle who worked at EMILY's List and who introduces me to Kate over email.

> On Dec. 5, 2016, at 12:50 PM, **Kira** wrote:
>
> Hi June,
>
> Here are some times that work for Kate this week, please let me know which one works best for you, or if you'd like me to list additional times the following week.
>
> Tues 12/6: 4:30pmET/1:30pmPT
> Wed 12/7: any window between 12pmET/9amPT and 3pmET/12pmPT
> Th 12/8: 1pmET/10amPT, 4pmET/1pmPT
>
> Thanks!
> Kira
>
> -----Original Message-----
> From: **Kate Black**
> Sent: Monday, December 05, 2016 3:33 PM
> To: June Diane Raphael; Michelle
> Subject: RE: book idea
>
> Hi June!
> Nice to meet you as well—I am looping in Kira who can help us find a time to connect this week!
>
> Best,
> Kate

I am already impressed and intimidated. Kate has a schedule and an assistant.

I had an infant son whose naps were a mystery and so I randomly chose a time and hoped for the best.

Hey there! It's me, Kate! I'll take the story from here!

I've spent over a decade working to elect women candidates and on policies that help women and families. I've worked on a presidential campaign as a political consultant, at the Democratic National Committee, at one of the biggest labor unions in the country, and at the largest resource for women in politics: EMILY's List. My career has been dedicated to electing more women to office, understanding why we need more women leaders, researching and communicating with women voters, and advocating for policies that benefit women and families. I have my master's in Women's Studies and focused on the intersection of women and political and public life in college.

So, as you could imagine, the 2016 elections had a tremendous impact on me. I had spent two years—and really, the bulk of my professional and academic career—working toward a moment when a woman could be elected president. After the election, I was not in a good place.

The loss had shook me hard. I was not sure what was next. . . .

But then June and I had our call and she told me about her idea: a fun, accessible, clever woman's guide to running for office. She asked if this type of book already existed. I said I didn't know of anything like it—and I thought I would know if it did.

We talked for more than an hour about her idea for this book and why it was so important. Needless to say, we went over our scheduled time. There was a lot to cover.

June and I talked about how women still represented just 23 percent of Congress and less than 28 percent of state legislatures. We talked about how in 2016 three women of color were elected to the US Senate—bringing the number up from one to four, the most in our country's history. An African American woman had not served in the Senate for nearly two decades until that point (not since Carol Moseley Braun from Illinois left the Senate in 1999). The first Latina ever to serve in the US Senate was also elected in 2016. We talked about these bright spots, but also the many barriers that exist for women looking to run for office—ranging from not being recruited to the high cost of campaigns. We talked about how, especially for young women, sometimes you can't be what you can't see. There are not enough women, especially women of color, at the table for us to think that we too can have a seat.

June's idea and that conversation were a breath of fresh air. They lifted my spirits in a way I had not expected, but so clearly needed.

By the end of the conversation I knew that Kate was not just a contact or resource. She was, in fact, the partner I needed.

And so here we are.

And here is our book. That's right, we just seamlessly transitioned into one voice. BET YA DIDN'T EVEN NOTICE! It's both of us now, here within these words! With our own font.

Thank you for joining us on this journey toward a representative government. Keep reading and stay working . . . we need you.

With love,

June and Kate

INTRODUCTION

Remember just a second ago when we called this piece of writing a book? Don't worry, it's still a book. But it's also a road map/tool kit/workbook/organizer—and a journal. It's chock full of the extensive knowledge Kate has accrued over years of working with women candidates and organizations committed to electing women. The granular details come from all of June's annoying questions that Kate had to answer. This book will help you pinpoint what's inspiring you to run for office (the beginning of your platform!) and figure out what position makes the most sense for you to run for. It will look at how running will impact your time, your family, your financial health, and your career or job. It'll show you how to determine how much money you need to raise, help you think about what to wear on the campaign trail, and tell you what you should do about the stuff about you on the Internet. Can one book do all those things, you ask? *YES, IT CAN—AND MORE!*

This book recognizes the hurdles women face. It acknowledges that the society we live, work, and love in was not built for women. It was not built to support working (both paid and unpaid) women. It was not built to support women of all colors, sizes, shapes, backgrounds, and bank accounts. But guess what? This book *was* built for women. This book understands that the details of a run for office can keep many women (maybe you, up until now) from trying. This book understands that because of the second and third shifts many of us are working, those details are EVERYTHING. This book understands that we need women both like you and unlike you in government.

By the end of the book you will be able to state clearly why you are running, what office you are running for and when, and most importantly you will know how a run for office will work . . . IN YOUR REAL LIFE.

By the end of this book you will have filled out this checklist. And you won't be alone while you do it. Throughout the book, six women politicians will share advice, words of wisdom, and warnings from their own time as candidates and

> ## DO NOT USE THIS BOOK AS A CRUTCH
>
> If you feel ready to run now, GO! Do not let the next webinar, training, meeting, *or this very book* keep you from starting your journey and running for public office. There are too many barriers in the world that hold women back from office (including access to financial networks; economic insecurity; gender, racial, and other stereotypes; and structural systems of oppression and power). This book should not be another one.
>
> And always remember: **Men. Are. Not. Waiting.**

I'm Running for Office.

THE CHECKLIST

1. I know why it's IMPERATIVE that more women run for office. ❑

2. I was nominated by _____.

3. Oh, hell yes, I'm qualified to run for office. ❑

4. I'm running for office to _____.

5. The office I'm running for is _____.

6. The filing deadlines for this office are _____.

7. The other requirements for this office are _____.

8. I have met those requirements. ❑

9. I've told these lucky people I'm going to run for office because making this promise to myself and others matters: _____.

10. I've completed my week of self-promotion. ❑

11. I've built my Campaign Supporter List in a good ol'-fashioned spreadsheet. ❑

12. My fundraising goal is _____.

13. I've done a full inventory of my online presence and set my damn privacy settings. ❑

14. When asked about any items found online about me (photos, arrests, etc.), I'm going to respond by saying: _____.

15. I absolutely know what I'm going to wear as a candidate. ❑

16. I've found the time to run for office. ❑

17. I've stared at the numbers and have figured out my financial plan to run for office. ❑

18. I understand how a run will impact my career. ❑

19. I have inventoried my self-care and caregiving, and I know how each will be sacrificed or safeguarded in my run. ❑

20. The incredible organizations I've contacted for help are _____
_____.

21. These are the women in my life I'm going to ask to run and buy this book for:

    WOMAN #1. _____   WOMAN #4. _____

    WOMAN #2. _____   WOMAN #5. _____

    WOMAN #3. _____

elected officials. We asked them questions to give you answers. They've been there, done that, and tell it like it is.

They are a mom, a millennial, an activist, a Republican. They are transgender, African American, Indian American, Latina. They serve in Congress and represent towns, cities, and state legislative districts across the country. Please sit your ass down as we introduce you to:

Washington Congresswoman Pramila Jayapal: Born in India, Pramila came to the United States BY HERSELF at age sixteen to attend college at Georgetown University.

Since she graduated, she's been a tireless advocate for those in need, whether she was working to provide health care for communities around the world, defending civil liberties following the 9/11 attacks, or advocating for immigrants' rights. She brought her drive for helping her community to politics when she was elected to the Washington State Senate in 2014, becoming the first South Asian American elected to the Washington State Legislature and the only woman of color in that legislative body. Then, in 2016, she ran and won a seat in Congress. She's used her voice in Washington not only to advocate for her home district in Seattle, but to make a difference on the national stage as well. From reducing student debt to combating the impact of climate change to fighting for a woman's right to choose, Pramila is an example of what happens when activism and passion marry public service.

Former Colorado State Speaker of the House Crisanta Duran: A sixth-generation Coloradoan, Crisanta's political life started early. Her father was a union leader and her mother was a state employee. Conversations around the dinner table focused on issues like affordable housing and wage rights (and probably also included some basic banter about passing condiments and second helpings). When Crisanta was fifteen years old, she traveled to Watsonville, California, to march on behalf of strawberry workers. After graduating from law school, she took a job as an attorney for the local United Food and Commercial Workers union.

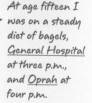

JUNE

At age fifteen I was on a steady diet of bagels, General Hospital at three p.m., and Oprah at four p.m.

Wanting to fight for the rights of workers on the state level, at the age of thirty, she ran and won a seat in the Colorado House of Representatives in 2010. At age thirty-three, she served as chair of the state's Joint Budget Committee. At age thirty-five, she spoke at the Democratic National Convention. And at age thirty-six, she was unanimously voted to serve as Speaker of the House, Colorado's first Latina Speaker, and the second youngest in history. In 2019, she announced her campaign for Colorado's 1st Congressional Dstrict. It seems reasonable to assume that by the age of forty she just might be leader of Earth and all its neighboring planets.

Mayor of Seattle Jenny Durkan: Jenny was born with big ambitions and into a big family. One of eight children, she was raised in Issaquah, Washington. After graduating from college, she taught English and coached girls' basketball in rural Alaska and then she headed to law school. In 2009, Jenny was appointed by President Obama as US attorney for the Western District of Washington. She became the nation's first openly gay US attorney. From her unanimous confirmation in 2009 to the end of her term in 2014, she was known for increasing federal capabilities to take on cyber-based threats, including a case involving a terrorist threat to attack a military recruitment office in Seattle.

In 2017, Jenny was elected the fifty-sixth mayor of Seattle and the first woman to lead the city in almost one hundred years. In office, she's worked to combat homelessness and signed Domestic Workers' Bill of Rights legislation into law. She's advocating for housing affordability, free college tuition, and criminal justice reform.

KATE

Maybe she's the reason everyone raves about Seattle; from what we hear, it rains all the time there.

Massachusetts Congresswoman Ayanna Pressley: Ayanna was raised by a single mom in Chicago. At a young age she was inspired by Shirley Chisholm and Barbara Jordan, and that inspiration turned into action. When she was just ten years old, she volunteered for her first campaign, working to elect Harold Washington as the first African American mayor of Chicago.

Ayanna attended Boston University, but left school and immersed herself in Massachusetts politics. At that time, she was entrenched in the issues of poverty, job creation, and advocating for women and girls—these same issues would become her platform for her successful city council campaign. In 2009, she became the first woman of color ever elected to the city council in Boston's history. As a councilwoman, she built coalitions to help ensure that students graduate high school and that women and people of color have accessible pathways to economic opportunities, and she strengthened services for families of homicide victims and sexual assault survivors.

In 2018, Ayanna announced her campaign for Massachusetts's Seventh Congressional District. Her slogan was "Change Can't Wait." She won the Democratic primary by defeating a ten-term Democratic incumbent. In January 2019, she was sworn in as a member of Congress, the first African American woman to represent Massachusetts in Washington. We cannot wait to see what Ayanna does next. Seriously, we have a very hard time waiting.

Columbus City Councilwoman Liz Brown: In October 2015, Liz participated in a debate for candidates running for city council in Columbus, Ohio. Most attendees knew Liz's background: she was raised in a suburb of Columbus, and had been active in Ohio politics and policy for most of her career. What the audience probably *didn't* know was that just seventy-two hours before the debate, she had given birth to her first child, her daughter Carolyn.

Nearly an hour into the debate, Liz had to leave to care for her newborn daughter. For Liz, paid family leave was not only personal, it was political—and a central theme of her work as a city councilwoman. Liz led the implementation of paid family leave for city employees in Columbus—the first of its kind in the Midwest and the third program nationally. Liz Brown blazed a path for herself as well as the pregnant and new moms who will come after her.

JUNE

I may have started ovulating while writing this.

Charlton Public Library Trustee and Charlton Town Constable Jordan Evans: When Jordan Evans was nineteen years old, she ran for the position of town moderator in Charlton, Massachusetts, a community of just fourteen thousand people. She didn't win that race. Or her next one for school board. But then she ran again and won, this time as state party delegate, a position that helped introduce her to policy makers and issues impacting the state.

In 2013, Jordan came out to a few close friends that she was transgender. Two years later, Jordan began transitioning and ran for library trustee. She won that election. The next year, she came out to her constituents. When she ran for reelection, she won again. Today, at twenty-seven, Jordan is the only openly transgender elected official in the Republican Party. Jordan has advocated to protect transgender student rights and fought alongside organizations to guarantee transgender nondiscrimination protections in Massachusetts. Anyone equally as inspiring at your local library?

No big deal, right? Just a few INSANELY IMPRESSIVE WOMEN. We've included their voices not only to inspire you, but also to remind you that at one point, these women were exactly where you are today: considering the idea of running for office.

And these are not the only women in this book! At the risk of overwhelming you with introductions, we want you to meet Heather, Shawnta, Monika, Beth, and Hilda. These five candidates are composites of real-life people who will be checking off their checklists as you check off yours. They will make the journey from deciding whether to run to figuring out the filing dates, assembling a campaign team, and beyond, right alongside you. Here are their questions and fears about running for office.

I'm Heather. I'm a proud Native woman, a mother, and a full-time nurse, and I take care of my elderly mother-in-law when I'm not at work. Do I have to quit my job to run for office?

Hi everyone, I'm Shawnta. I'm a veteran, the founder of a nonprofit, and a recovering alcoholic. I'm running for city council and have no idea how much money I'll have to raise. HELP!

My name is Monika (with a k). I'm a first-generation immigrant, a millennial, a lesbian, a barista, a ride-share driver, and a babysitter. I'm barely making ends meet. There is no way I can afford a run for office—right?

I'm Beth. I'm Asian American and divorced. As a recently retired local news anchor, I'm well-known in my community. I've been asked a number of times to run, but I've always put it off because I've felt I wasn't qualified. I'm still not sure I am.

Hey, I'm Hilda. My oldest daughter is being bullied online and I desperately want to change the way the school system deals with this. I am a full-time mom and am worried I won't have enough time to run for office.

Do you have similar questions or anxieties? Do you see yourself in any of these characters? You may look like one of them, or a mixture of them, or none of them. If you don't identify with any of these women, don't worry, because the great news is that your authors are representative of all women and between them have incredibly diverse backgrounds of race, sexual preference, political preference, age, and economic status.

Not.

We are two white women.

JUNE

I'm a white cisgender heterosexual woman who is married to a man. I'm in my thirties and a registered Democrat. Also, I'm alarmingly attractive.

Me too!

KATE

Sure, there are tons of differences between us: June has two young children; Kate just had her first baby. Kate works in politics and government; June is an actress, writer, entrepreneur, and activist. Kate is from the Midwest; June is from the East Coast. Kate has standards when it comes to the TV shows she watches; June does not.

But when it comes to thinking about all women and how they might approach a run for office, we are simply two white women thinking about how all women might approach a run for office.

This lack of diversity between us is the most glaring when we consider one of the biggest barriers women face when running for office: access to wealth. Along with the other identities we share, we also grew up with roughly the same amount of wealth and now enjoy roughly the same amount of personal wealth and access to people with wealth.

And there is another way we are the same.

We are not just committed to getting more women into office. We are committed to getting more women of color, more LGBTQIA women, more women with disabilities, and more lower-income women into office. We are writing this book for *all* women, even as we recognize and acknowledge that this book can't possibly encapsulate every woman's experiences, insights, and challenges. We don't presume to speak for every woman. We can't. But we proudly acknowledge here that:

1. We are committed to dismantling the white dominant, patriarchal society that is in place, while recognizing that we are a part of it and have benefitted from it. Not sure what this means? Flip to page 231, and read "White Privilege: Unpacking the Invisible Knapsack" by Peggy McIntosh.

2. We are both Democrats and have worked to elect Democratic women to office. We also acknowledge that we will not get to gender parity in our government without Republican women, and we hope that they will read this book and run for office.

3. We have never run for office. Yet. However, we have both considered running for office. June woke up on Election Day 2016, imagined the possibility, and is never saying never! For Kate, running for office is a long-term goal.

4. We have worked our hardest to think about EVERY woman when writing this book. We did our best to avoid including language and images that might be oppressive to our readers, but our best may not be good enough.

Examining our own identities and privileges has complicated our thinking in the best possible way, making us more compassionate and more engaged—and more committed to electing a representative government!

TO THAT END, KEEP READING AND STAY WORKING.

We need you.

"If you don't have a seat at the table, you're probably on the menu."

—SENATOR ELIZABETH WARREN (D-MA)

Chapter One

WHY IS IT IMPORTANT THAT MORE WOMEN RUN FOR OFFICE?

What Are Our Current Numbers?

★

How We Got Here: A History

★

Why Representation Matters

When you think of our government, what comes to mind? Is it:

Most of us likely answered A. If you answered B and imagine that our government is run by literal fat cats roaming the hallways with hundred-dollar bills in their mouths, this book might not be for you.

We are betting that most of you did not choose C. Most people believe that our government is composed of a bunch of older white dudes.

That's because our government IS composed of a bunch of older white dudes.

"So what?" you might say. Maybe you didn't pick up this book to change the landscape of our government. You might only wish to change the landscape of your town by adding more public gardens. That's cool. However, by simply holding this book and considering a run for office, you are a part of the history of women in politics. We can learn a lot about our own campaigns from looking at both the historical moment we are in and also where we came from.

So where are we at when it comes to women's representation in government?

NOT AT THE TABLE

America has been a country for coming up on 250 years. Women have had the right to vote for almost 100 years. Right now, women make up 50.8 percent of the US population. So . . . we should probably make up half of Congress? Or at least a third of it? Right?

Nah.

Here are some charts, if you are a chart person.

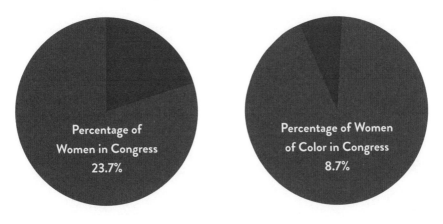

That's right. As of 2019, 23.7 percent of Congress is made up of women. Of 535 people in Congress, only 127 are women and only 47 are women of color. That's 8.7 percent of the entire Congress.

There are only 4 women of color in the United States Senate.

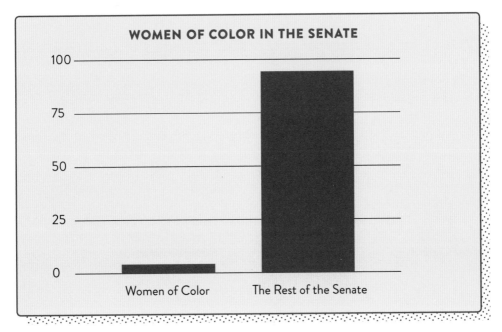

And three of those four women were just elected in 2016! In the words of President Trump, "SAD!"

And here's the starkest number of all the stark numbers. Hold on to your hats, ladies.

79.

Sounds like a good number, right? Not when it's where we stand in terms of women's representation in federal government in the world.

Out of nearly two hundred countries, we rank 79th.

Here are the top ten countries when it comes to women in federal government:

1. Rwanda (61 percent)

2. Cuba (53 percent)

3. Bolivia (53 percent)

4. Mexico (48 percent)

5. Sweden (47 percent)

6. Grenada (47 percent)

7. Namibia (46 percent)

8. Costa Rica (46 percent)

9. Nicaragua (45 percent)

10. South Africa (43 percent)

11–78. LOTS OF OTHER COUNTRIES THAT ARE NOT TOUTED AS THE LEADER OF THE FREE WORLD!

79. United States of America (23.7 percent)

And it's not just on the federal level. Women are underrepresented at all levels of government.

Let's say that again in bigger type . . .

Women are underrepresented at all levels of government.

State legislatures do a bit better than Congress, but not much. Women hold just 28.7 percent of all seats in state legislatures. Women are only 22 percent of mayors in cities with over 30,000 people.

And there are 20 states—almost half the country—that have never been represented by a woman governor.

KATE

This is big. Governors hold tremendous power over the laws in our states—they influence everything from funding for schools to funding for new roads and bridges to emergency preparedness. Oh, and by the way, more governors have become president than senators or other office holders.

And, shockingly, women's marginalization extends from government into almost every sector of our society. In 2017, women made up the majority of minimum-wage earners; overall, women working full time were paid 80 cents to the dollar compared to non-Hispanic white men. African American women were paid 61 cents, Asian American women were paid 85 cents, white, non-Hispanic women were paid 77 cents, Native Hawaiian and other Pacific Islander women were paid 59 cents, American Indian and Alaska Native women were paid 57 cents, and Latinas earned just 53 cents for every dollar paid to white, non-Hispanic men. And according to the *New York Times*, in 2018, there were fewer women CEOs of Fortune 500 companies than there were CEOs named James.

Are you wondering how many grim statistics two women can throw at you? If you can believe it, we actually pulled back so that you wouldn't put down this book and walk directly into your oven. There is clearly a problem. And it's a big one. But the good news is that you are here. And you are the solution. And you aren't alone. You are joining a lineage of women who have also decided to do one of the bravest things a woman can do: raise their hand and be a part of the solution.

Crisanta Duran,
Former Colorado State
Speaker of the House

As Colorado's Speaker of the House, a lot of the time I was the only woman or the only person of color in the room, as well as the youngest. Although I think that there was significant progress in 2018, we still have a lot more work to do to make sure that our elected officials are representative of the population as a whole.

A HISTORY OF WOMEN'S SEATS AT THE TABLE

If we promise you a ton of pictures, will you stay with us for a history lesson? We are desperate to put Kate's master's degree in women's studies to use. Finally.

In order to know where we need to go to be fully represented, we need to know where we've been and also how far we've come. We also need to recognize where feminism has been problematic, divisive, and exclusionary. First-wave feminism's (from approximately 1848 to 1920) "Votes for Women" didn't mean "Votes for All Women." Women of color were routinely left out of the white, mostly upper-class fight for suffrage. This didn't stop after the 1920s. We could call second-wave feminism (from around 1963 to the 1980s) "white middle-to-upper-class feminism" instead. Many women followed Betty Friedan, author of *The Feminine Mystique*, out of the house and into the workforce. But many women were already in the workforce doing low-paying work and were left wondering what "feminism" could do for them. The third wave (started in the 1990s), which some would argue we are still in, has brought us intersectionality and "we should all be feminists" T-shirts. It has also seen the first female major-party nominee lose the 2016 presidential campaign. It seems that in many ways women appear closer to one another than ever (read: the Women's March, #MeToo, Time's Up) and that in many ways we couldn't be further apart (read: a majority of white women voted for a sexual predator for president).

So how did we get here? The incomplete history we present is both inspirational and a cautionary tale. We know that without the women we mention below we probably wouldn't be writing this book. But we also know that these are not the only voices that have shaped our world. We are blown away by these women (especially those who were doing this work in the damn 1800s), and we are also critical of many of them, whose narrow view of "women" left many women out. We contain multitudes!

AN INCOMPLETE TIMELINE OF WOMEN'S POLITICAL POWER IN THE UNITED STATES (AND SOME OTHER CRUCIAL DATES)

WHERE WE MUST START

WE BEGIN WITH AMERICAN INDIAN WOMEN LEADERS. We must honor their history and acknowledge how little of it is recognized and how important it is to examine its erasure. While Americans learn about and celebrate Christopher Columbus (and ignore the death, disease, and turmoil he brought with him), we do not learn about the Native women who were here and leading their people long before Columbus sailed the ocean blue. As American Indian Movement leader Carter Camp wrote, "Many, if not most, of our nations were matriarchal so of course their leadership was made up of women. However, the Christian invaders could not understand it and would not deal with women leaders so they chose a male Chief and spoke only to him. The real women leaders' names never appeared in the history of the tribes, which was/is written by the invaders."

1776 ABIGAIL ADAMS ASKS HER HUSBAND TO REMEMBER THE LADIES, OR ELSE.

While her husband, John, is at the Continental Congress in Philadelphia, Abigail Adams writes him asking that he "remember the ladies" in the "new code of laws" he and other men were creating. If women's legal rights were not improved, Abigail warned, "we are determined to foment a rebellion, and will not hold ourselves bound by any laws in which we have no voice or representation."

1838–40 THE ANTISLAVERY MOVEMENT SPLITS AND, UH-OH, IT'S BECAUSE OF WOMEN'S PARTICIPATION.

When a woman named Abby Kelley is appointed to the business committee of the American Anti-Slavery Society, the society freaks out and splits itself into three different groups: one made up of radical abolitionists and women's rights supporters, one exclusively male, and one that relegated women to fundraising and fundraising only. And a complicated history between the women's movement and the movement for racial equality is born.

1848 SUFFRAGETTES ORGANIZE IN THE UNITED STATES.

The Seneca Falls Convention, the first women's rights convention in the United States, is organized by Elizabeth Cady Stanton, together with Lucretia Mott, Martha Coffin Wright, Mary Ann M'Clintock, and Jane Hunt. The attendees issue the Declaration of Sentiments, which insists that women "have immediate admission to all the rights and privileges which belong to them as citizens of these United States." This, the first women's rights conference in the United States, left out and ignored the oppression faced by black women.

Lucretia Mott

1851 SOJOURNER BRINGS THE TRUTH.

A leader in the abolitionist and women's suffrage movement, Sojourner Truth delivers her "Ain't I a Woman?" speech at the Women's Rights Convention in Akron, Ohio.

"AIN'T I A WOMAN?"

Sojourner Truth's speech was in response to men in the audience claiming that women were weak. She said:

"That man over there says that women need to be helped into carriages, and lifted over ditches, and to have the best place everywhere. Nobody ever helps me into carriages, or over mud-puddles, or gives me any best place! And ain't I a woman? Look at me! Look at my arm! I have ploughed and planted, and gathered into barns, and no man could head me! And ain't I a woman? I could work as much and eat as much as a man—when I could get it—and bear the lash as well! And ain't I a woman? I have borne thirteen children, and seen most all sold off to slavery, and when I cried out with my mother's grief, none but Jesus heard me! And ain't I a woman?"

1872 THE FIRST WOMAN RUNS FOR PRESIDENT.

Victoria Claflin Woodhull becomes the first woman to run for president—her platform focuses on women's suffrage, regulation of monopolies, nationalization of railroads, and an eight-hour workday. Here are three other things to know about her: she attended school on and off for only three years before she dropped out; she worked as a traveling clairvoyant; and she and her sister were the first female stockbrokers on Wall Street.

1916 MONTANA MAKES HERSTORY.

Jeannette Rankin (R-MT) becomes the first woman elected to Congress. After winning a seat in the House of Representatives, she says, "I may be the first woman member of Congress, but I won't be the last." Notably, Montana was one of the first states to grant women the right to vote, in 1914.

1920 WOMEN WIN THE RIGHT TO VOTE NATIONWIDE.

After protests in the streets and in front of the White House, marches, arrests, and imprisonment, the movement for women's suffrage makes progress in states and in Congress. Alice Paul and other leaders of the suffragette movement celebrate the ratification of the Nineteenth Amendment to the Constitution, ensuring women's right to vote.

1933 FIRST WOMAN NAMED AS LABOR SECRETARY.

Frances Perkins becomes the first woman to serve in a presidential cabinet, as secretary of labor under President Franklin D. Roosevelt. She is instrumental in creating the New Deal, which established the minimum wage, worker protections, and Social Security.

1941–45 ROSIES ARE RIVETING.

Women's participation in the labor force increases significantly during World War II, setting the scene for future generations of Rosies.

    The first image of Rosie the Riveter was created in 1942 by J. Howard Miller, an artist in Pittsburgh. Rosie went on to become a symbol of American women's empowerment and determination to succeed.

1957 REACHING NEW HEIGHTS.

Dorothy Height, whom President Barack Obama called the "godmother of the Civil Rights Movement," becomes president of the National Council of Negro Women and serves until 1997. In 1963, she is one of the key organizers of the March on Washington, working alongside Martin Luther King Jr. In 1971, she cofounded the National Women's Political Caucus.

1962 DOLORES FORMS FARM UNION.

Dolores Huerta and Cesar Chavez form the National Farm Workers Association, which later becomes United Farm Workers, the first successful farm union in the country.

1963 EQUAL PAY NOW.

Congress passes the Equal Pay Act, which prohibits paying anyone differently for the same work based on their sex. The law is spearheaded by Congresswoman Edith Green, a Democrat from Oregon, and Katharine St. George, a Republican from New York.

1964 HAMER FIGHTS FOR FREEDOMS.

Fannie Lou Hamer, a leader of the Mississippi Freedom Democratic Party (MFDP) addresses the Democratic National Convention and calls for the MFDP to unseat the all-white Mississippi delegation. During her testimony, she details the violence she and others faced when attempting to register to vote. At the end of her testimony she asks, "Is this America, the land of the free and the home of the brave, where we have to sleep with our telephones off the hooks because our lives be threatened daily, because we want to live as decent human beings, in America?"

1964 CIVIL RIGHTS ACT BECOMES LAW.

Congress passes the Civil Rights Act of 1964. The bill is debated in Congress for over five hundred hours. Title VII of the act prohibits employment discrimination based on sex, race, color, religion, or national origin.

1965 COURT RULES COUPLES CAN CHOOSE TO USE BIRTH CONTROL.

KATE

Yes, you're reading that correctly. A Supreme Court case about the right to use condoms, diaphragms, or any kind of birth control. Hands off my rhythm method, please.

The Supreme Court rules on *Griswold v. Connecticut* and establishes a right to privacy in a case challenging a Connecticut law that prohibited the use of contraception, including for married couples.

BRING U.S. TOGETHER

VOTE CHISHOLM 1972
UNBOUGHT AND UNBOSSED

1972 SHIRLEY RUNS.

New York Democratic congresswoman Shirley Chisholm runs for president. She is a woman of many firsts:
* ★ The first African American congresswoman
* ★ Founding member of the Congressional Black Caucus and the National Women's Political Caucus
* ★ The first woman to run for the Democratic Party's presidential nomination

JUNE

"Unbought and unbossed" is the best campaign slogan ever.

1972 TITLE IX PASSES.

Congress passes Title IX of the Education Amendments of 1972, which prohibits discrimination on the basis of sex in any federally funded educational program. The bill is co-written by Congresswoman Patsy Mink, a Democrat from Hawaii (and also the first Asian American woman to serve in Congress).

1973 *ROE V. WADE* IS DECIDED; WOMEN'S HEALTH PROTECTED.

The Supreme Court, still all white men, rules in the landmark case of *Roe v. Wade*, establishing a woman's right to legal abortion.

1980 FLORIDA WOMAN SERVES IN SENATE.

Florida Republican senator Paula Hawkins becomes the first woman elected to the US Senate in her own right. (She did not succeed her husband or father in the position, as previous senators had.)

1981 O'CONNOR BECOMES FIRST FEMALE SUPREME.

Nominated by President Ronald Reagan, Sandra Day O'Connor becomes the first woman to serve on the Supreme Court.

1984 FERRARO FOR VEEP.

New York Democratic congresswoman Geraldine Ferraro becomes the first woman nominated to be vice president on a major party ticket. (Also in 1984, Mississippi gets around to ratifying the Nineteenth Amendment, giving women the right to vote. Little late to the party?)

1985 EARLY MONEY IS LIKE YEAST—IT MAKES THE DOUGH RISE.

EMILY's List, an organization dedicated to electing pro-choice Democratic women, is founded by Ellen R. Malcolm.

1985 INDIGENOUS WOMEN'S NETWORK ACTIVATED.

Activist Winona LaDuke cofounds the Indigenous Women's Network, an organization dedicated to uplifting and empowering Native women's participation in political, social, and cultural systems.

1986 MIKULSKI BEGINS HISTORIC TENURE IN SENATE.

Maryland's Barbara Mikulski is the first Democratic woman elected to the US Senate in her own right. She goes on to serve until 2017, becoming the longest-serving woman in Congress.

1987 WILMA MANKILLER IS FIRST WOMAN ELECTED TO HEAD MAJOR AMERICAN INDIAN TRIBE.

In 1985, the principal Chief of the Cherokee Nation resigned. Wilma took the helm. Then, in 1987, she ran for the seat and was elected the first woman principal Chief.

1992 THE YEAR OF THE WOMAN.

Historic numbers of women run for office and a record number of women are elected to serve in Congress: four new women to the Senate and more than twenty new women to the House.

1993 RBG!

Ruth Bader Ginsburg is appointed to the Supreme Court, and we've never been the same.

1993 FAMILY AND MEDICAL LEAVE ACT PASSES.

Congress passes the Family and Medical Leave Act, which provides twelve weeks of unpaid leave for new parents and for personal and family illnesses.

JUNE

Get ready for a good old-fashioned LOL. Which developed countries offer paid family leave? ALL OF THEM BUT OURS!

1994 VIOLENCE AGAINST WOMEN ACT BECOMES LAW OF THE LAND.

Congress passes the Violence Against Women Act, authorizing funds for services for victims of domestic violence and rape.

1997 FIRST OF MANY (WELL, ACTUALLY JUST A FEW) FEMALE SECRETARIES OF STATE.

Madeleine Albright becomes the first female secretary of state, blazing the trail for future secretaries of state Condoleezza Rice and Hillary Clinton.

2007 INTRODUCING MADAM SPEAKER (ROUND 1).

Nancy Pelosi becomes the first woman Speaker of the House. Upon getting the Speaker's gavel, surrounded by her grandchildren, she says, "For our daughters and granddaughters, today we have broken the marble ceiling . . . the sky is the limit."

2008 FIRST GOVERNOR, NOW SENATOR.

New Hampshire Democrat Jeanne Shaheen is the first woman to be elected as both a governor (in 1996) and a senator (in 2008). Also, bonus! The New Hampshire Senate becomes majority female.

2008 PALIN NAMED VP ON GOP TICKET.

Alaska Governor Sarah Palin becomes the first woman to run for vice president on the Republican ticket.

2009 FIGHT FOR EQUAL PAY CONTINUES WITH LILLY LEDBETTER.

The Lilly Ledbetter Fair Pay Act passes Congress. The bill, sponsored by Senator Barbara Mikulski, helps victims of pay discrimination recover lost wages.

2009, 2010 SOTOMAYOR AND KAGAN NAMED TO SCOTUS BENCH.

In 2009, Sonia Sotomayor is confirmed to the Supreme Court, becoming the first Latina justice. In 2010, Elena Kagan becomes the fourth woman to sit on the Supreme Court.

2012 FIRST OPENLY GAY SENATOR WINS.

Democrat Tammy Baldwin is elected as the first openly gay senator in history. (She also becomes the first female senator from Wisconsin.)

2016 MORE WOMEN THAN EVER SERVING IN CONGRESS.

Congress has the most women ever: 105. Three women of color are elected to the US Senate, including Catherine Cortez Masto, the first Latina senator. And in Oregon, Democrat Kate Brown becomes the first openly bisexual person to win a gubernatorial campaign.

2016 HILLARY WINS POPULAR VOTE.

Hillary Clinton is the first woman to become a major party's nominee for president. She loses the electoral vote, but wins the popular vote, with more than 65 million people voting to elect her to the most powerful seat at the table.

JANUARY 2017 FOUR MILLION WOMEN MARCH.

Women organize and lead the largest single-day demonstration in history. Four million women—and men and children—march all over the world. In big cities and small towns, women join together to march not just in protest of Donald Trump's election, but in solidarity for the future they are fighting for.

NOVEMBER 2017 AND THEN THEY RUN.

Women don't just march. They run—and win. In Virginia, women, including several first-time candidates, win eleven seats in the state House of Delegates, including the first transgender woman, the first Asian American woman, and the first Latinas. New Jersey voters elect Sheila Oliver as their first woman of color lieutenant governor; Vi Lyles is elected as the first African American woman mayor of Charlotte, North Carolina; and Jenny Durkan becomes Seattle's first lesbian mayor.

APRIL 2018 FIRST SENATOR GIVES BIRTH WHILE IN OFFICE.

Illinois Senator Tammy Duckworth becomes the first senator to give birth while in office. Duckworth's bringing her newborn daughter to work served (in her words) to "bring the Senate into the twenty-first century by recognizing that sometimes new parents also have responsibilities at work." Sometimes big changes come in small sizes (with the perfect little hat).

MAY 2018 EQUAL RIGHTS AMENDMENT GAINS MOMENTUM.

Illinois becomes the thirty-seventh state to ratify the Equal Rights Amendment (ERA) and joins
the movement for establishing women's equal rights in the Constitution. Congress initially set a
deadline for ratification by 1979, then extended it to 1982. Legal experts suggest the deadline could
be extended again. At least thirty-eight states need to ratify the amendment for it to be enacted.
That's right, thirteen states haven't ratified it; we just need one more, so we're looking at you, Alabama,
Arizona, Arkansas, Florida, Georgia, Louisiana, Mississippi, Missouri, North Carolina, Oklahoma, South
Carolina, Utah, and Virginia.

NOVEMBER 2018 WOMEN WIN AT HISTORIC LEVELS.

A record-breaking number of women run for office in 2018: 53 women run for the Senate and
476 women run for the House. When the primaries are over, 257 women appear on congressional
ballots in November—a record high. Because of this record number of women candidates, an
unprecedented number of women win their races and serve in office in 2019: 102 women serve
in the House, 25 in the Senate, 9 women serve as governor, and over 2,100 women serve in state
legislative offices across the country.

2019 AND BEYOND WOMEN REJECT "YEAR OF THE WOMAN" AND BEGIN "CENTURY OF THE WOMAN."

[Insert Your Name Here] joins a massive wave of women running for office and changing the face of
our government. Parity is no longer a dream but a reality. Women fully control their own reproductive
rights. Poverty is stamped out. The environment returns to its natural balance. The world is at peace.

WHY IT'S SO IMPORTANT TO BE AT THE TABLE

Before we continue, rest assured that we know that all women don't vote the same, think the same, or act the same just because they identify as women. Don't worry, we aren't going to fall into the essentialist trap we have set up for ourselves. Just identifying as a woman does not ensure that:

★ You will govern on behalf of women.

★ You will govern well.

★ You will govern the same as other women.

★ You will win the votes of all women.

We have all seen disastrous women candidates and elected officials. However, we believe that a diverse, reflective, and representative government is the best government.

And there is research that shows that women's leadership and representation in our government makes a difference.

Have a clean set of panties to change into before you read these facts about the importance of women leaders.

1. Women lawmakers sponsor more legislation than their male counterparts. In fact, women sponsor about three more bills every two-year session than men. This might be because women are also more likely to collaborate and work together, so naturally, they get more shit done.

2. Women are more likely to focus on and pass legislation on issues like education, reproductive rights, civil liberties, and health care than men. And women are more likely to focus on bills that impact women, such as legislation addressing sexual discrimination, equal pay, children and family issues, education, social services, and health care.

3. Over time, women bring 9 percent more federal spending home to their districts than their male counterparts. How much does 9 percent matter? A lot. Think about all that federal funding provides: school construction, public health centers, building and maintaining roads and bridges, health care for children, school lunches, foster care, and affordable housing for our communities.

Here are just a few examples of what some women electeds have been up to in the early aughts and then some.

★ In 2017, the Leon County School Board in Florida—which is 100 percent women, by the way (amazing, amiright?!)—unanimously amended the school district's anti-bullying policy to extend to bus stops and bus rides. The policy also included protections from retaliation for anyone who filed a bullying complaint and protected over twelve thousand students who ride the bus in the district.

★ As director of Indian education at Montana's Office of Public Instruction, Denise Juneau created an American Indian curriculum for Montana schools. Then, in 2008, she was elected Montana's state superintendent and became the first American Indian woman to hold state-wide office in the nation.

★ In 2013, famously wearing pink running shoes, Texas state representative (and later gubernatorial candidate) Wendy Davis held an almost thirteen-hour filibuster to protect women's access to abortion. She stood up for the rights of Texas women for hours with nothing to eat, drink, or lean against. She couldn't go to the bathroom or tap someone else in while she took a break. She spoke until almost midnight before she was ruled out of order. The crowd, which had grown to fill the entire House chamber, cried out: "Let her speak!" The bill she protested ultimately passed, but her act sparked a national conversation about women's reproductive health.

Wendy Davis during her filibuster

Though our numbers are disturbingly small, women electeds have been making a huge impact. Imagine what we could accomplish with more of us in office.

Now on to the next step: **making sure you get a seat at the table.**

KEEP READING. STAY WORKING.

We (clearly) need you.

I'm Running for Office.

1. I know why it's **IMPERATIVE** that more women run for office. ❑

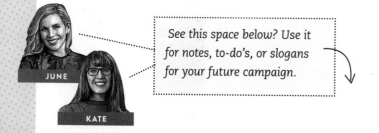

See this space below? Use it for notes, to-do's, or slogans for your future campaign.

She Believed She Could, SO SHE DID

Deb Haaland

When European colonizers first came to North America, they met the nearly one million American Indians who were already here. In 1776, the United States was formed, yet the government did not grant citizenship to American Indians until 1924. While American Indian men have served in Congress, not a single Native woman had. Until Deb Haaland and Sharice Davids (both were elected in 2018).

Deb, a member of the Laguna Pueblo tribe, represents a progressive district in New Mexico. Her campaign focused on restoring funding for American Indian programs. She said, "I'm not under the belief that I can represent any tribe or even my own tribe, but what I can do is make a seat at the table available to tribal leaders to speak from their own voice."

Deb's career has always focused on the underrepresented. She led the passage of legislation to allow members of New Mexico American Indian tribes to receive in-state college tuition. She worked with LGBTQIA allies to pass a state ban on conversion therapy. And she worked to elect progressive candidates across New Mexico. In fact, she was the first American Indian woman to chair a state political party.

A single mom who put herself through college and law school—and who still had college loans to pay off—Deb knew what it was like to struggle to make ends meet. That's why she campaigned on a platform of raising wages, paid family leave, affordable health care, free childcare and pre-kindergarten, and funding for social services for tribes.

When Deb won her primary, she said, "I'm not exceptional. I didn't grow up with privilege. I almost feel like my winning is a shout-out to democracy everywhere." We agree, Deb. We so agree.

"I'm sometimes asked when will there be enough [women on the Supreme Court] and I say, when there are nine."

—SUPREME COURT JUSTICE RUTH BADER GINSBURG

Chapter Two

DOESN'T SOMEONE HAVE TO NOMINATE ME?

You're Already Nominated

★

How Did It Feel?

What's the best way to get a woman to run? Ask her! And then ask again! Research has found that we need to ask women to run for office, and usually more than once.

But here is the great news for you, Dear Reader. *You are already nominated.* You've already been asked. By merely having this book in your hands you have been nominated to run for office (either by yourself or by someone else). The hardest part is over! (Well, not quite, but the first part is over!) The beginning of your leadership story has already been written.

You are probably holding this book for one of the following reasons:

★ **YOU BOUGHT IT FOR YOURSELF.** Yes! Yes! Yes! You just did one of the bravest things a person can do. You nominated yourself to run for public office. You are offering the world your talent and your gifts and your confidence. Seeing yourself as a leader and having the courage to put yourself out there is arguably the most important step in this process, and you've done it. Congrats!

★ **SOMEONE GAVE IT TO YOU.** Well, damn. Someone in your life believes in you so much they think you should run for office! That's meaningful. It seems that you've been nominated, my friend.

★ **YOU ARE A MAN WHO WANTS TO RUN FOR OFFICE AND YOU CAN'T FIND THE RIGHT BOOK.** Boy, bye.

Okay, now that it's just us gals, we can move on to our first question. How did it feel to be nominated?

Write your answer here, please: _____
_____
_____
_____
_____

Did you write . . .

I feel amazing and I'm raring to go.

I want to throw up.

It's the craziest thing I've ever heard. Is Ashton Kutcher about to pop out of a closet to tell me "You've been punk'd," because this is a hilarious joke.

I'm confused, angry, and overwhelmed.

No matter what the feeling . . . it's okay.

It's definitely okay to think running for office is the craziest damn idea you've ever heard.

It's not crazy to have internalized a lot of the negative messaging and direct discrimination that's been hurled at us, oh, our whole lives. It's not crazy to think that running for office is insane and should be left to others. But it would be crazy to let these thoughts stop you.

It's also okay to think this is an amazing idea and that you are just the person to do it. Because yes, you are.

It's okay to be excited about running for office. It's okay to be a little scared about running for office. And it's also okay to feel angry about someone even suggesting this idea to you. If you are thinking, "The world is an unfriendly and frankly dangerous place for me, I'm a trans African American woman who lives in rural Alabama. Voters in my community are never going to support me," to you we say, your candidacy is vital. We can't be what we can't see, which is why you need to be seen. That is a lot to put on one person, we know. And we acknowledge that it may not be safe for you (emotionally or physically) to enter the public arena. And you should absolutely consider that. But right now, we're asking you to work the book. We're hoping by the end you will have the resources and support you need for your candidacy,

Remember Monika, Heather, Shawnta, Beth, and Hilda, the women who are composites of real-life women candidates? Here's how they felt about being nominated:

MONIKA

After hearing me complain about the current administration's stance on immigration pretty much all day every day, my girlfriend told me I had to stop talking about it and do something about it. She told me I needed to run for office. And that felt . . . FUCKING CRAZY!

As a Native American woman, I've gotten very involved in issues involving my community, and my two sons joined me in the protests at the Dakota Access Pipeline. They know how passionate I am about everyone having access to health care and that it's something I want to see happen in my lifetime. When they asked, or rather demanded, that I run for office . . . well, it moved me more than I can express.

HEATHER

SHAWNTA

I nominated myself! The problem I want to fix is so simple I couldn't wait around for someone else to do it. It felt great to take some action.

This isn't the first time someone's asked me to run, and to be honest it always makes me so anxious. I feel sick.

BETH

HILDA

My husband and I have both been beside ourselves trying to get our daughter some help from being bullied online, so when he asked me if I would consider actually running for the school board I felt . . . relieved. Maybe this will be the way to ease her pain.

Your nomination might bring up a lot of different feelings. Maybe all the feelings? Here's the thing: It doesn't matter if you nominated yourself or someone else nominated you. The good news is that you are nominated! Whether you've dreamed of being president since you were a little girl, or had never considered elected office till recently, no matter. You've begun the journey, and that's what matters.

KEEP READING. STAY WORKING.

We need you.

I'm Running for Office.
THE CHECKLIST

1. I know why it's IMPERATIVE that more women run for office. ❑
2. **I was nominated by** _____.

She Believed She Could,
SO SHE DID

Vi Lyles

In 2017, Charlotte, North Carolina—the Queen City—elected its first African American mayor: Vi Lyles.

Vi was born and raised in Columbia, South Carolina, but always dreamed about living and working in Charlotte, the big city that was just an hour away. She got her chance when she became one of the first African American women to attend Queens College (now Queens University). While there, she realized that the challenges she experienced in her segregated community in South Carolina existed in Charlotte too. She committed herself and her career to making Charlotte a better place for her, her children, and her community.

Vi's forty years of public service (first as a budget analyst for the city, then later as budget director and assistant city manager) prepared her for her role as mayor, but it was two major events in Charlotte that drove her to run: when the state legislature overturned a local protection of the city's LGBTQIA community and the fatal police shooting of an African American man.

During her mayoral campaign, Vi advocated for affordable housing, economic opportunity, improved public safety, and rebuilding trust between police and Charlotte's citizens.

In 2019 she said, "I've had a really wonderful career. I've raised a family and have grandchildren now. . . . But yet, every day I think how can I grow to be better, and what could I've done differently to make sure that we deliver on our commitment to the people who live in our city that it will be a place where they will be able to function and work and live. I think about that a lot."

"When women apply for a job, we ask ourselves, 'Am I qualified? Do I have the experience? Do I have the education? Do I have the abilities?' When a man looks at that job, he thinks, 'How much does it pay?' We need to stop second-guessing our abilities. We need to stand up and make ourselves heard."

—SENATOR CATHERINE CORTEZ MASTO (D-NV)

AM I QUALIFIED TO RUN FOR OFFICE?

Women vs Men on "Qualifications"

Your Experience Is Your Expertise

The Résumés of Current Leaders

We can almost hear you telling us, "Okay, fine, I was nominated, but that doesn't mean I'm actually qualified to be an elected official!" Women often feel like they are underqualified for the job. And men? They do not feel this way.

According to a 2011 study titled "Men Rule: The Continued Under-Representation of Women in US Politics," conducted by Jennifer Lawless and Richard Fox, when asked, men were almost 60 percent more likely than women to "assess themselves as 'very qualified'" to run for office, and women were "more than twice as likely as men to rate themselves as 'not at all qualified.'"

What's more, not only do more men believe they are qualified to run for office than women, **but a majority (55 percent) of the men who said they were NOT qualified would still consider running.**

If you are more of a story person (June) than a numbers person (Kate), then here is a scene we wrote for you recapping this phenomenon.

MEN: Overall, we assess ourselves as "very qualified" to run for office.

WOMEN: That's interesting. We are way more likely than you (actually more than twice as likely!) to say we are NOT QUALIFIED.

MEN: For real? That's funny because even among those of us who DON'T think we're qualified to run for office, more than half would still consider running.

MEN WHO DON'T THINK THEY ARE QUALIFIED: Oh, we for sure would!

WOMEN: Hmph.

Hmph indeed.

YES, YOU ARE QUALIFIED TO RUN FOR OFFICE.

Women, it is time to assume the confidence of mediocre men! Let's just go ahead and assume (like so many bros) that it's our right to do so. Let's let go of all of our preconceptions of what an elected official is supposed to be. And if you can't do that so easily, then fine. We are here to challenge those preconceptions and convince you that you are already qualified.

Check off what you think the résumé of a qualified politician should look like.

❏ Ivy League–educated

❏ Lawyer

❏ Graduate degree(s)

❏ Wealthy

❏ Previous experience in government

❏ A standing tee time at your local country club

If you checked off all of the above, think again. Let's look at the 115th Congress (2017–18) to see what their résumés looked like prior to entering Congress. Yes, there are lawyers in the bunch, but there are also:

★ 101 members who have worked in education, including professors, teachers, instructors, counselors, and coaches

- ★ 26 farmers, ranchers, or cattle farm owners

- ★ 14 doctors, including 3 dentists and 3 veterinarians

- ★ 10 members of the military reserves and 6 members of the National Guard

- ★ 9 social workers

- ★ 8 ordained ministers

- ★ 8 engineers

- ★ 7 radio talk show hosts

- ★ 6 car dealership owners

- ★ 5 police officers, 3 sheriffs, 1 police chief, and 1 firefighter

- ★ 3 union representatives

- ★ 2 Peace Corps volunteers

- ★ 2 nurses

- ★ 1 optometrist

- ★ 1 CIA agent

- ★ 1 microbiologist

JUNE

Seems like a hell of a lot of car dealership owners, but what do I know?

KATE

True! But think about it—they understand how to communicate with people, how to make their pitches, and how to present their ideas clearly and with passion. How else did so many people buy the PT Cruiser?

You can see that the people on this list weren't all lawyers and career politicians, and yet they were *still* qualified candidates. In fact, their varied professional backgrounds and experiences were assets, not liabilities.

Ayanna Pressley,
Massachusetts Congresswoman

My biggest challenge was to get out of my own way and not to allow insecurities and self-doubt to stand in the way of what I had to contribute. Like many women, I constantly questioned if I was ready, if I was smart enough, or if I had done enough in the world. Ultimately, I came to the realization that running for the city council was simply a continuation of the public service I had done throughout my life. And I was "qualified" to run, mostly because I had the desire to serve and because my lived and professional experiences would make me an empathetic and effective leader.

YOUR EXPERIENCE IS YOUR EXPERTISE

The first words of our Constitution are "We the People." It's nice to remember that those "people" are made up of all of us "people." Not just lawyer people (love them as we do). People like:

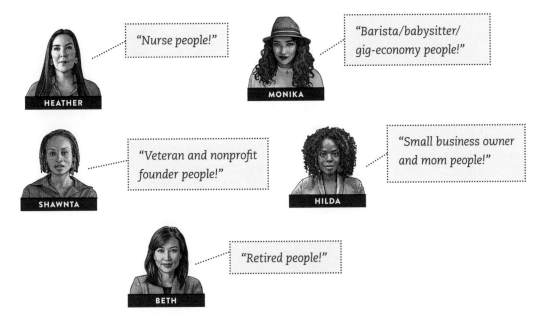

HEATHER — "Nurse people!"

MONIKA — "Barista/babysitter/ gig-economy people!"

SHAWNTA — "Veteran and nonprofit founder people!"

HILDA — "Small business owner and mom people!"

BETH — "Retired people!"

All of these people should have their voices heard, whether it's in Congress, in the statehouse, in city council, in town assembly, or beyond. The kind of people you are is the kind of people we need in office.

You are qualified just by being you. Your experience is your expertise. Let's say that again:

Your experience is your expertise.

Your story and your voice are what will make the difference in an election, not a variety of degrees or previous job titles. Would it help to have a killer résumé? Sure. But do you need one to run for office? No! It's not about the work you've done, or what school you went to. It's about how your life experience has shaped your worldview and has informed your vision for the future. Ultimately, voters will connect with you because of you and your story.

Here are three amazing women whose experience became their expertise when they ran for office.

★ **Veteran and Senator Tammy Duckworth (D-IL)** was raised in Southeast Asia by her Thai mother and American father. When she was in high school, her family moved to Hawaii. She attended the University of Hawaii and joined the ROTC as a graduate student. In 2004, she was deployed *Her experience* → to Iraq. On November 12, 2004, her helicopter was hit by a rocket-propelled grenade and she lost her legs and partial use of her right arm. After recovering from her injuries, she became an advocate for veterans. She worked to implement programs to help those suffering from post-traumatic stress disorder, to improve traumatic brain injury screening, and to reduce homelessness among veterans. She explained the reason she ran for Senate in 2015, writing, "The next time we go *Her expertise* → to war, we should truly understand the sacrifices that our service members and the American people will have to make. Which is why, when my colleagues start beating the drums of war, I want to be there, standing on my artificial legs under the great Capitol dome, to remind them what the true costs of war are."

★ **Former Chief of Police, now Congresswoman, Val Demings (D-FL)** was born in a two-room home in Jacksonville, Florida. The youngest of seven children, she was the first in her family to graduate from college. She began her career in public service as a social worker, and in 1983 she moved to Orlando to join the police force. She graduated as class president of the police academy and worked up the ranks while she raised her family. In 2007, she became *Her experience* → Orlando's first female chief of police.

As chief, she founded a mentorship program for at-risk students and rejuvenated Orlando's most crime-ridden housing complex by expanding access to social services like childcare, a GED program, and job-skills training.

She first ran for Congress in 2012 but lost by four points. When she ran again *Her expertise* → in 2016 on a platform that included criminal justice reform and economic opportunity, she said, "Tragically, we have seen far too many incidents across this country involving the police and the community that did not have to happen. And I'm talking about a profession that I was proud to serve, a profession that I love. I know the dangers for law enforcement officers . . . but we always have to make sure we're doing it right."

She defeated her opponent by thirty points.

★ **Rancher, Former Congresswoman, and Governor Kristi Noem (R-SD)** worked

from a young age on the family farm, caring for cattle and horses and helping with the harvest. When she started college, her father passed away in a farming accident, and *Her experience* ← Kristi returned home to work on the farm and ranch full-time. In 2006, Kristi decided she could help other small businesses and entrepreneurs by serving in public office. She ran for state representative and won. In her second term, she became assistant majority leader in the state legislature, where she served until 2010, when she ran for Congress. She won a narrow race to take South Dakota's only seat in the US House of Representatives. After her election, she talked about her message for small business owners, farmers, and ranchers, saying, "I ran on the campaign that we needed smaller, more limited government, we needed to cut our spending, we needed to make some tough decisions to make sure small businesses could still survive and exist. And that resonated across South Dakota."

Her expertise

These women have done amazing things, and their stories are incredible. Monika, Beth, Hilda, Heather, and Shawnta have amazing stories too. They are not lawyers, and they have not served in public office before. And they are qualified to run, just as you are.

"Jesus, I get it, I'm qualified!" you say. "But aren't there some actual requirements?"

We will dive into the exact office you are running for and what the requirements are in Chapters Five and Six. But our point is this: requirements and qualifications are different.

The only thing you *need* to be to run for office? You.

Jordan Evans,
Charlton Public Library Trustee

It doesn't matter whether you're running for city council or US Congress, because when you run for anything, you're representing yourself in the hope that people will believe in you enough to let you represent them too. Now more than ever, the world needs more strong women, and that means you!

KEEP READING. STAY WORKING.

We need you.

I'm Running for Office.

THE CHECKLIST

1. I know why it's IMPERATIVE that more women run for office. ❑

2. I was nominated by _____.

3. Oh, hell yes, I'm qualified to run for office. ❑

Use this space to jot down your experience—and your expertise.

She Believed She Could, SO SHE DID

Susana Martinez

Susana Martinez's political philosophy was shaped by caring for her sister, Leticia, who has cerebral palsy. Susana and her sister were born in El Paso, Texas. Her father was a boxer who went on to become the deputy sheriff in El Paso and then started a security business. Her mother was a telephone operator and bookkeeper. Susana and Leticia were raised in public housing before moving to a blue-collar neighborhood. When their mother passed away, Susana became Leticia's legal guardian. Advocating for her sister, who relied on government support, led Susana to politics. "Lettie is on Medicaid," she explains. "I believe in providing services to adults and children who can't take care of themselves."

Growing up, Susana was always argumentative—so much so she had the nickname "*la abogadita*," or the little lawyer. It was no surprise that she went to law school and quickly got a job working as a prosecutor. She then won an election for district attorney, going on to win high-profile cases involving sexual and child abuse.

Then, on her fiftieth birthday, in 2009, she decided to run for governor. Knowing she could help people like her sister in New Mexico, she stepped up and put her name on the ballot. Her campaign focused on rooting out corruption and bringing more transparency to government. It paid off—in November 2010, Susana became the first Latina governor in US history and New Mexico's first female governor. While in office, she focused on education, being tough on crime, and expanding Medicaid. Her time as governor ended in 2018. What's next for Susana? Committed to being an inspiration for women and girls, she says, "I have to deliver the results I promised, because as the first Hispanic female governor, I'm going to pave a path of some kind. I want it to be one that little Hispanic girls will want to follow."

"People sometimes ask how I can run for Congress when I have four children. I tell them I have four children, how can I not?"

—CONGRESSWOMAN MIKIE SHERRILL (D-NJ)

WHY AM I RUNNING?

What Fires You Up?

★

How to Channel That Energy into
Your Future Campaign

★

Practice Your Pitch

Want to know a truly *amazing* fact about women candidates? While men usually run for office as part of a logical career path, women usually run to solve a problem in their communities. Are we saying women are selfless, not concerned with ego, and are all-around the superior sex? No—but maybe kinda? Feast your little peepers on these three women who ran for office to solve a problem they saw.

★ **New Hampshire Senator Maggie Hassan** says her son, Ben, who has cerebral palsy, is the reason for her political career. She first ran for office after fighting to make sure Ben was accommodated in his public elementary school.

★ **Rhode Island Governor Gina Raimondo** first ran for office because the state budget forced cuts to public libraries. As the founder of the state's first venture capital firm, she knew a thing or two about investing smartly. She ran for state treasurer to fix the pension system, creating room in the budget to protect the libraries she cared so much about.

★ **Former Utah Congresswoman Mia Love**'s Saratoga Springs neighborhood was so overrun by midges (flies about the size of mosquitoes) that her neighbors were afraid to go outside for fear the bugs would rush into their homes. Mia went to the developer of her subdivision to demand they help get rid of the infestation. It was called the "War of the Midges," and Mia won. She went on to become a city councilwoman, then the mayor. In 2014, she became the first black Republican woman and the first Haitian American elected to Congress.

JUNE

MOTHERFUCKING MIDGES!

For these women, the personal was political. Now it's your turn. What are the issues that fire you up? What about the status quo are you passionate about changing? Where are the midges in your life?

WHY ARE YOU RUNNING FOR OFFICE?

Let's investigate the "why" of your run—the issues you care about, the problems you wish to solve, the change that you demand. We are going to name those problems, and we're going to figure out how you've been showing up for them so far. Then we're going to write your elevator pitch: a short, engaging sentence or two about who you are, why you're running, and what you want to run for. It's going to look something like this.

My name is _____*,*

and I'm running for office to _____

As you consider what really grinds your gears, know that this short pitch will become more fleshed out and eventually transform into your platform. When you win your race, it will evolve into your agenda.

If you aren't sure yet what office you're running for, it may feel crazy to figure out the "why" before you know the "where." But trust that there is a reason we're asking you these questions in this order. We want this chapter to inform the next (where you'll nail down what office is the best fit for you). Also, identifying why you want to run at this early stage in the process will help push you to make this dream a reality. As we must do when experimenting with new sexual positions AND running for office . . . trust the process.

Let's begin by figuring out your top three issues/causes/problems and why you chose them. To give you a sense of how others answered these questions, here's what Shawnta and Hilda had to say. First up: **Shawnta.**

SHAWNTA

For me, it's a no-brainer! **VETERANS' SERVICES:** *I was an ROTC student in college and graduated right before 9/11. I was deployed to Afghanistan and served for three years until I was injured in the line of duty. When I came back home, my physical recovery was much harder than I had expected, and I turned to alcohol to numb myself. Getting the health care necessary after returning to civilian life (for both physical recovery and addiction treatment) was a nightmare for me and many other vets that I know.* **AFFORDABLE CHILDCARE:** *Childcare for my one-year-old daughter costs more than my rent. This is unaffordable, and I know many other moms in the same position.* **EMERGENCY ACCESS:** *When my mom fell in her home, the ambulance couldn't get up her narrow street because cars were parked on both sides. When you need help, emergency vehicles need to be able to get to you fast.*

And here's what **Hilda** had to say:

HILDA

They say the personal is political, and for me, it couldn't be more personal.
ONLINE HARASSMENT AND BULLYING: *My oldest child faced harassment online from other kids in her school. As a parent, I felt completely helpless watching her self-esteem and academic performance drop because of it.*
SUPPORT FOR TEACHERS: *I'm a mother of two kids in public schools (and to another little one who will head there in a few years). I'm involved in the PTA and know how hard teachers work. They are underpaid, their class sizes are too big, and they are not getting the support they need from their schools.* **SMALL BUSINESSES CAN'T SUCCEED:** *I had to close my design company because of the high business taxes in California. Ultimately, my dream was paralyzed by the high rates.*

Your turn. The three issues I care most about/problems I want to fix are:

1. _____

_____

_____

2. _____

_____

_____

3. _____

_____

_____

Great! You've completed a crucial first step.

Now let's look at how you are showing up to solve these problems. For the moment, we are going to leave tweeting, retweeting, and posting articles out of the equation.

Before we turn the focus on you, let's look to **Shawnta** for some inspiration:

SHAWNTA

VETERANS' SERVICES: *I started a nonprofit to solve this problem and am its executive director! The organization helps veterans navigate the VA system to get the health care they need, whether it's for physical recovery from an injury, treatment for substance abuse, or accessing mental health care.* **AFFORDABLE CHILDCARE:** *Beyond trying to solve my own childcare needs with my mother's help, I haven't addressed this problem in a bigger way.* **EMERGENCY ACCESS:** *I've petitioned the city to change the double-sided street parking to one-sided street parking on my mom's street and other narrow streets like it.*

Here's how **Hilda** showed up:

HILDA

ONLINE HARASSMENT AND BULLYING: *I went to my kid's teachers. I met with the superintendent. I brought this to a PTA meeting. But everyone is telling me that because the bullying is happening off campus, it's out of the school's jurisdiction. These are all kids she knows from school. There has to be something the school can do.* **SUPPORT FOR TEACHERS:** *I started a supply drive for teachers at our school so they wouldn't have to pay for supplies out of their own pockets.* **SMALL BUSINESSES:** *Because I know how hard small businesses have to work to stay afloat, I try to shop local and small any chance I get. Not shopping on Amazon is HARD WORK when you have small kids.*

Now you go! How have you shown up to solve the problems you see?

1. _____

_____

_____

2. _____

_____

_____

3. _____

_____

_____

**Pramila Jayapal,
Washington Congresswoman**

I always thought that I was best on the "outside" as an activist. . . . Ultimately, I realized that after fifteen years of trying to get others in office to do the things I thought needed to be done, it was high time I ran myself. I realized that elected office was simply another platform for organizing and we needed to have more organizers from the movement in elected office, more women, and more women of color in particular.

Are you looking at what you just wrote and realizing you aren't showing up in a meaningful way for certain issues? If you aren't actively doing anything to find solutions, what can you do to change that? How can you get involved in finding solutions to the issues you care about?

If you're thinking, "I'd like to, but I don't know how," rest assured that there are lots of ways to get involved. Civic engagement can mean different things to different people—you can start by reading and educating yourself further on the issues you care about, or you can grab a friend and jump right into a rally. The most important thing is that you put your bod where your mouth is in whatever way you can.

What follows are some civic engagement suggestions. This is not an exhaustive list—there's no way we could know about all the groups and activities in your community. Some are general ideas; other suggestions are more specific. Either way, our hope is that this list sparks some ideas about ways you can start showing up for the issues you care about most.

★ **VOTE. VOTE. VOTE. VOTE.** In every election.

★ Show up at your town hall or city council meetings.

★ Check out the volunteer opportunities at your church, synagogue, mosque, or other place of worship.

★ Is there a candidate you believe in who's already running for office? Volunteer for her campaign!

★ Figure out the best way to support the homeless population where you live. Can you help at a food bank? Start a food drive? Donate clothes and/or toys?

★ Go to your union's meetings.

★ Show your support for a cause you care about by bringing your bod to a rally or march. Add to the numbers by showing up.

★ Call your representatives and ask to sit down and talk with them about problems that need fixing.

★ Get involved with, go to meetings of, or volunteer with groups you care about or want to know more about, like the Humane Society, ACLU, NAACP, Clean Water Action, American Association of University Women, Planned Parenthood,

Black Lives Matter, Moms Demand Action, Indivisible, Sister District, Flippable, MomsRising, PFLAG, Sierra Club, League of Women Voters, RepresentUs, and CASA in Action, for starters.

★ Is the environment your primary focus? In what ways can you personally make your life greener? Consider taking public transportation or biking, buying locally produced and/or recycled clothing and goods, adding solar panels to your home, or composting.

★ There are tons of organizations that foster mentorship between kids and adults. What skills can you offer?

★ Does voter suppression make your heart pound and your blood boil? Lots of state and nationwide organizations work to ensure that every American who wants to vote can.

Showing up for causes you care about can expose problems you weren't aware of. It can, in fact, inspire your entire campaign, and, dare we say, your life's work! So if you haven't been showing up, guess what? It's time to.

WRITE YOUR PITCH

So, you've figured out what you care about, why you care about it, and what you've been doing so far to create change. Now you're going to write your pitch—a quick, hot take on who you are and why you're running for office. You'll say this pitch a million times. "A million?" you say. "Yes, a million," we say. You will be telling literally every single person you meet that you are running for office.

For instance, at the bank:

"Hello, are you making a deposit or withdrawal, and from which account?"

"A withdrawal from checking, please. I'm Jane Smith and I'm running for city council to . . ."

. . . or the grocery store:

"Paper, plastic, or did you bring your own bags?"

"I brought my own, and by the way, hi, I'm Jane Smith and I'm running for city council to . . ."

. . . or the coffee shop:

"Would you like extra foam on your pumpkin spice latte?"

"You know it, and also I'm Jane Smith and I'm running for city council to . . ."

See? You can seamlessly work it into every conversation you have! Let's hear from Heather, Monika, Beth, and Shawnta on what they wrote for their pitches. And we want to remind you, it's okay to not know where you are running yet. For the sake of this exercise, you can just say "for office."

My name is Heather and I'm running for office to make sure everyone—no matter what they look like, where they live, or what they do—has access to affordable, quality health care. As a nurse, I see too many families come into the ER who can't afford the care they need. Health care is not a luxury and no one should have to sacrifice to stay healthy.

My name is Monika, and I'm running for office to ensure that immigrant families are not only protected but represented in our government. My family and I immigrated to America almost twenty years ago, and I know firsthand what the needs of this community are. I plan to be their voice in office on issues ranging from protecting workers' rights to ensuring that all kids get access to high-quality education throughout the city to boosting legal aid for those who need it—regardless of immigration status. (Okay, that was long and I'm going to have to practice it a few times!)

My name is Beth, and I'm running for office to protect Iowa consumers. Payday lenders, big banks, debt collectors, and insurance scammers have taken advantage of hardworking Iowan families, farmers, and seniors for too long. I've reported on these stories, and now I'm running to continue my fight against abusive companies.

My name is Shawnta, and I'm running for office to solve a problem that keeps me up at night: My elderly mother lives in a house that ambulances cannot access. I'm running to make sure all residents have access to city emergency services.

You might be surprised to see that Shawnta, whose life's work is centered around advocating for veterans, is not running for office to work on veterans' issues. Yes, she's passionate about that issue, but another problem presented itself that she knew she could fix in office.

These are their pitches as of today. That doesn't mean that in a week, a month, or a year—or five years—they will be the same. As Heather, Monika, Beth, and Shawnta learn more about the issues they care about and talk to more people, they might refine and hone their pitches. The same goes for you. As time goes by, your views might change. That's okay. Actually, it can be more than okay. Your thinking and self-expression evolving can be pretty fucking cool.

You can come back to your answers and your message over and over again. But the task right now is to express where you are today, to tell the world (and yourself) why you want to run—what's making your heart soar and your blood boil, what problems you see, and how you can solve them.

Let's do this—now write your pitch.

Liz Brown, Columbus City Councilwoman

I found it awkward and self-important to pitch a crowd on my personal merits. To get over this, I tried to focus instead on our shared values.

My name is _____ and I'm running for office to _____

_____

_____

_____

_____

_____

_____

_____.

AWESOME. KEEP READING. STAY WORKING.

We need you.

I'm Running for Office.

THE CHECKLIST

1. I know why it's IMPERATIVE that more women run for office. ❑

2. I was nominated by _____.

3. Oh, hell yes, I'm qualified to run for office. ❑

4. **I'm running for office to** _____.

JUNE

KATE

Got an idea for a logo? Draw it here.

She Believed She Could, SO SHE DID

Ilhan Omar

When Ilhan Omar was eight years old, she and her family fled Somalia's civil war, spending four years in a refugee camp in Kenya before emigrating to the United States. They lived first in Virginia, eventually settling in Minnesota.

Just a few years after arriving in the United States, Ilhan attended political meetings with her grandfather and translated for him what was being said. It was there that her commitment to her community and public service began. She went on to work as a policy aide, a community health care educator, and as the director of a group focused on promoting women from the East African diaspora to be leaders in their communities.

In 2016, just over two decades after arriving in the United States, she ran for a seat in the Minnesota state House. Her platform was based on what she described as "justice and the common good." She ran on affordable education, investments in mental health, and criminal justice reform. On election night, she became the first female Somali American Muslim lawmaker in the United States.

When Congressman Keith Ellison announced his plan to run for Minnesota attorney general, Ilhan decided to run for his open seat. She campaigned on a platform that included Medicare for all and raising the minimum wage to $15 an hour. In November 2018, she made history again by becoming the first Somali American in Congress and one of the first Muslim women in Congress. Previously seeking refuge from a war in Somalia, she is now United States Congresswoman Ilhan Omar.

"We're here to help people, and if we're not helping people, we should go the fuck home."

———

—SENATOR KIRSTEN GILLIBRAND (D-NY)

WHERE AM I RUNNING, FOR GOD'S SAKE?

MEET YOUR MATCH: AN OVERVIEW OF OFFICES YOU CAN RUN FOR

Here's a fact most people don't know: **there are more than 500,000 public offices you can run for in the United States. Over 500,000.** Not just the 435 seats in the US House of Representatives or the 100 seats in the US Senate, or even the 50 governorships. There are secretaries of state, state legislatures, county boards, city councils, school boards, and so many more offices that you—yes, you!—can run for.

If you already know where you are going to run, more power to you. Feel free to skip ahead to the next chapter. But if you are unsure what seat you want to claim, or are deciding between a few, keep reading this chapter. It's nice here in this chapter. At the very least, it will provide you with a basic civics lesson. At the very most, it will help you identify which office best solves the problems you laid out in Chapter Four. That's right—we are going to match the problems you want to fix to the office that's best able to do so. For example:

A GOOD MATCH!		A NOT-SO-GOOD MATCH!	
The Problem You Want to Solve	**The Office You Decide to Run For**	**The Problem You Want to Solve**	**The Office You Decide to Run For**
People drive way too fast around schools in my town. We need more speed bumps and traffic control so people SLOW THE F DOWN.	City Council	Countries are taking advantage of the United States' open borders and fair-trade policies and we're losing well-paying American jobs in the process.	Director of Library Services

KATE

NOPE! Try Congress, please!

Before we go further, a quick word about salaries. Some elected positions pay a salary, some do not—and among those that do, the amounts vary widely. Are we saying that you should choose the office that pays the most? No. But we *are* saying you should know all the financial facts about the office you're planning to run for. Does it pay a living wage? Or do you have to have a second job to make it work?

Do not be surprised if you are appalled by how low some of the salaries are. This is because voters typically don't support elected officials who vote to give themselves a raise, and conventional wisdom also has it that low pay will deter career politicians. But what has happened is that salaries for many elected positions are so low (we're talking $100-a-year low, in one state) that it keeps people from being able to afford to serve. Leadership shouldn't be a luxury. Yet one more problem that needs fixing! We'll look deeper at how to afford a run for office later in Chapter Twelve. For now, trust that there is help ahead on how to afford running for office.

Okay! Now let's get back to finding the perfect office for you. As you read through this chapter, (circle) every elected position that piques your interest.

LET'S START LOCAL

Local offices are based in your town, city, or county. Ever wonder who decided to plant those flowers around the village green? Or who you should thank for finally repaving DeMott Avenue? It's most definitely one of your local-ass politicians.

Local elected officials work directly with residents to solve problems and effect change right in their own towns and counties. There are tons of reasons to give a local run some serious thought. Local elected officials know firsthand the challenges their communities are facing, and more important, they also understand the solutions. They know their constituents, often on a first-name basis, and they can bring about tangible change that impacts everyday lives. What's more, getting your start in local politics can help grow your political muscles, learn more about the issues, and expand your network. Who knows? Starting locally could always lead to the next opportunity.

It's important not to be deceived by the word "local." Local does not always mean the town council meetings in Stars Hollow (*Gilmore Girls*, anyone?), where everyone attends and discusses plans for the upcoming harvest festival. Local can mean the school board of Seattle (with seven members making decisions that affect more than 50,000 kids), the mayor of Austin (which represents nearly 1 million people), or the city council of New York City (with 51 members representing 8.5 million residents). In short, size does matter here. A bigger city or town could mean more people to serve, more resources to help people, and may mean a bigger salary and a bigger staff, which means more people helping you achieve your goals. In addition, if you're running in a big local race, it may mean you'll have to raise a significant amount of money, maybe even as much as you would in a federal race.

Here's a snapshot of some local offices. Reminder: circle the ones that interest you.

SCHOOL DISTRICTS

★ **Number of Offices:** 95,000 school board positions you can run for in the nation. Let's say that again: 95,000 elected offices in school districts.

★ **Only Parents Allowed?** No—having children in a public school is not a requirement. Do you pay property taxes? Then you should care about what happens in schools!

★ **What Problems Do These Offices Solve?** School boards can decide everything from the books read in classrooms to requirements for arts and music classes. Members of school boards oversee school construction and collective bargaining agreements with teachers and staff. Want to make sure teachers are paid a fair wage? Do you care about that new elementary school being built in your neighborhood? The people who solve these problems are members of the school board. Don't fuck with them.

SPECIAL DISTRICTS

★ **Number of Offices:** 84,089 offices, including fire control, library services, roads, and sanitation—just to name a few. All of these fall under the category of "special districts" providing very localized services to meet specific community needs.

★ **What's So Special?** As communities grow, they may decide that they are lacking a specific service, or maybe the level of service they are receiving isn't what it should be to meet the growing needs of their town. Hello, special districts. These are public entities that can be created to meet specific, *special* needs. That might include fire districts, park services, sanitary districts, or water districts.

★ **What Problems Do These Offices Solve?** Does your town have an infestation of mosquitoes that must be taken care of, or else? Running for commissioner of the mosquito control district is a real thing. Do you think your town needs more fire trucks or more volunteer firefighters? You could be the next chairwoman of the local fire district. Is that trash piling up because collection happens only on Saturdays in your town? You could be the director of its sanitation district. And the world would know not to fuck with you.

COUNTY OFFICES

★ **Number of Offices:** 58,818 offices across more than 3,000 counties. Offices you can run for include sheriff, supervisor, district attorney, tax collector, and clerk.

★ **What Problems Do These Offices Solve?** Are you enraged by the stories of excessive and often deadly police force used against unarmed African American men and women? Sheriffs can propose body cameras for police departments. They can hire more people of color and demand bias training. They can also focus on community policing. Are you a lawyer who wants to protect and defend your community in court? Perhaps you should look into the district attorney's seat. Do you care deeply about everyone paying their fair share of taxes? Tax collector might be the job for you. These are county officials. Don't you dare fuck with them.

TOWN GOVERNMENT

JUNE

* **Number of Offices:** 126,958 offices in more than 16,000 towns. Elected positions include members of the board of selectmen, the planning board, and the board of health.

Gendered language alert! If you are a selectwoman thinking of running to be a selectman, maybe it's time to also change the title of the position?

* **What You Might Be Asking Yourself:** What do folks on the board of selectmen do? They help run the town! They figure out what time the libraries close, they bring events to the town, they decide when the town fair will be. They are select, and they are men or women!

* **What Problems Do These Offices Solve?** Did a giant sex toy store open on Main Street? The town government probably okayed it. Members of the town government make the decisions about the future of the town—how it will function and how it will grow. Are you super passionate about city planning and whether your neighbor can pop up that third story onto their home? Maybe the zoning board is for you. If you want to make sure restaurants are keeping up with the health code, the board of health would be a great place to start. Do not fuck with them. Seriously.

MUNICIPAL OR CITY GOVERNMENT

* **Number of Offices:** 135,531 elected offices across nearly 20,000 cities and municipalities. Positions may include: mayor, city council member, city auditor, and city comptroller.

* **Is This Like *Parks and Rec?*** The city council members (the mayor sometimes being both a member of the council and the head of the council) function as a congressional-style legislative body. What in the hell does that mean? They essentially propose bills, hold elections, and pass laws that govern the city.

* **What Problems Do These Offices Solve?** Is your main street riddled with potholes? Are the schools in your area crumbling and in need of repair? Does your city need more bus routes for commuters? Mayors and members of the city council deal with issues ranging from fixing potholes (yes, please!) and funding capital improvement projects to setting property taxes. Do you want to bring more transparency to government? City auditors run investigations and make sure tax dollars are being used smartly and efficiently. This is city government. It's best not to fuck with them.

If you had told me a few years ago that I would someday run for office, I would've assumed that I'd be running for Congress to demand more federal aid for veterans. I definitely would not have believed you if you told me I'd be running for city council to make sure all streets were safe for ambulances and emergency vehicles. And yet here I am. I know that as a city councilwoman I can solve this problem. And that feels awesome.

SHAWNTA

I had a terrible experience with my local school board, which is why I had my eye on filling a seat there. So my decision on what office to run for was easy. For now, this is a local issue, but if I'm successful, who knows?! Maybe I'll run for a seat on the state education board next!

HILDA

City council makes perfect sense for Shawnta. And school board, for now, solves the problem that Hilda sees.

Which of these local offices we just listed match the problems you want to solve?

Now fire up that Google machine and find out whether these offices exist in your community. There may be issues of nomenclature. Is the county clerk actually called the "county recorder" where you live? Does the sheriff also do tax collection in your town? Each community is different, so titles and responsibilities may differ from town to town.

What specific offices in your town match the problems you want to solve? _____

STATE-LEVEL OFFICES

State-level offices work to enact policies that impact residents of the state. Think about it—each state has its own unique challenges to face. For instance, North Carolina, South Carolina, Georgia, and Florida have to deal with hurricane season and therefore have laws in place to assist with mass evacuations and emergency responses during storms. And in states like Indiana, Iowa, and Illinois, agriculture and farming are top industries, so protecting against pollution and ensuring fair business practices for farmers is a state priority. State officials may be elected by their district and represent their communities, or they may be elected statewide. Elected leaders take stock of the issues and opportunities impacting their residents and work to pass laws that make sense for them.

Do I Need to Move to [Insert Your State Capital Here]? Well, you might not have to move, but download your podcasts, because even if you don't, you will be commuting to the capital city to do your job. Among the requirements for being a part of the state legislature is *working from the capitol*. It's where votes happen and where business gets done.

Below you will find a list of elected state positions. Keep your pen by your side to circle offices that you think might match your goals. And remember, these are state officials. It would be wise not to fuck with them.

STATE LEGISLATURES

★ **Number of Offices:** 7,382 offices in state Houses and state Senates across the country. Terms vary by state.

★ **Why Would I Want to Work in the State Legislature?** To get shit done. Legislation moves more quickly at the state level than at the federal level. Bills are introduced 23 times faster than they are in Congress. Even better, 19 percent of state Senate bills and 13 percent of state House bills are actually voted on, passed, and signed into law—compared to just 3.6 percent and 1.9 percent of US Senate and House bills. So, to repeat: if you want to enact change NOW, get thee to the state legislature.

★ **What Problems Do These Offices Solve?** Are you for or against the death penalty? It is legal in some states and not in others. Some states are passing laws that directly challenge *Roe v. Wade*. Does that fire you up? If so, then think about running for state legislature. Do you think plastic grocery bags are destroying the environment? Some states have banned them altogether. If your belly is burning on these issues, then off to the state capital you go, not to be fucked with.

STATE BOARDS

★ **Number of Offices:** 1,331 offices.

★ **What Exactly Is a State Board?** Think your local school board but representing the entire state. State boards set overarching educational policies that instruct municipalities on how best to operate.

★ **What Problems Do These Offices Solve?** Do you believe that in order to graduate from high school in your state, every student should be required to take gym and art classes? As a member of the state board of education, you could establish graduation requirements for the state. You could also set curriculum guidelines. For example, if you believe that schools should teach the FAIR Curriculum (an experientially based curriculum that encourages an understanding of social injustice), you might think of running for state board of education.

STATEWIDE ELECTED OFFICES

★ **Number of Offices:** 1,036 openings available on variable terms across all fifty states. Offices can include governor, lieutenant governor, attorney general, or comptroller.

★ **Would It Be Appropriate to Call a Governor the Queen of the State?** No, it would not. The governor, however, is the head of the executive branch of the state and has power over the state budget and appointment of officials. In some states, he or she can commute pardons and is the commander-in-chief (at times) of the state's National Guard. She can veto state bills and, in many states, has her own residence (think White House, but on a state level). Reminder: twenty states—almost half the country—have *never* been represented by a woman governor.

Where there's a governor, there's also a lieutenant governor. In some states, you can run for the position; in others you are chosen to be on a ticket (like the vice president). Lieutenant governors are the next in line of succession to the governor's office. In some states, they preside over the state legislature and can break tie votes in the state Senate. Lieutenant governors can lead special-issue task forces, run boards and commissions, and help move the governor's agenda forward.

The attorney general represents the state in legal matters. The secretary of state helps run the state's elections and oversees voter registration procedures. "Hey, what about comptroller?!" you may ask. How dare we forget about comptroller! Do you get a weird thrill out of balancing your checkbook? This might be the job for you. The comptroller makes sure money is going into and out of state coffers appropriately and essentially balances the checkbook. Now that's a person not to be fucked with.

This list of statewide offices is far from exhaustive. Find out what's available in your state by using the almighty Google.

★ **What Problems Do These Offices Solve?** These are the top dogs in state government. Do you want to establish statewide mandates requiring computer science classes in every elementary school to get more girls into STEM? Or do you want to lead the fight to raise the minimum wage in your state? Maybe you want to start a commission to combat opioid addiction and open treatment centers across the state? Are you jonesing to file legal briefs suing the federal government over its immigration policies and DACA? All these things can be done by statewide elected officials. We beg of you, do not fuck with these people.

BETH

The reason I'm so interested in running for governor is because, among other things, protecting consumers from fraud and abuse affects all Iowans, not just a handful of people in one town or city.

Anything at the state level sound interesting to you?_____

_____

_____

_____

FEDERAL OFFICES

Welcome to Washington! You can run for a seat in the US House of Representatives or the US Senate, and of course for President of the United States (as you know, you have to be asked to run for veep). If elected to Congress, you will work most days in Washington, DC, but travel to and from your district frequently—think almost every weekend (it's a lot of driving and/or airline miles).

CONGRESS

★ **Number of Offices:** 535. In the House, there are 435 seats up for reelection every two years. In the Senate, there are 100 seats (two from each state) up for reelection every six years.

★ **Welcome to Our Nation's Capital:** Whether you represent your district or your entire state, your vote not only represents your community, but also impacts the entire country. Senators and Representatives vote on national policy issues like education, health care, immigration, and whether or not to send troops into battle.

★ **What Problems Do These Offices Solve?** Do you believe we need a bigger military presence around the world? Do you think our Social Security system needs to be reformed? Do you want a say in which judges get appointed and confirmed to the federal bench and the Supreme Court? Members of Congress vote on everything from naming post offices (seriously) and deciding how Americans get health care to protecting our national security. These 535 individuals constitute the legislative arm of our country, direct the nation's domestic and foreign policies, and perform checks and balances on the other branches of government. We wouldn't fuck with them.

EXECUTIVE OFFICE

★ **Number of Offices:** Two—president and vice president. Term: four years, with the possibility of being reelected for an additional term.

★ **What Room Shape Do You Prefer?** Must be okay with working in an oval-shaped office.

★ **What Problems Do These Offices Solve?** The president of the United States signs bills into laws, enacts executive orders, leads our military, and directs the federal government to carry out her vision for the future. Sounds like a big job, right? Well, that's because it is. When each president is sworn into office she promises to protect and defend the Constitution of the United States. Every day the president and her team work to ensure that each American has the right to life, liberty, and the pursuit of happiness. What that looks like is up to each president—what will it look like when it's your turn?

> **WHAT WOULD I GET PAID?**
>
> Most members of Congress are paid $174,000, and that helps cover the costs of maintaining a home in their district and in DC (though some very frugal members of Congress sleep in their offices to cut down on costs—true story). If you're a member in leadership (think Speaker of the House), you earn more. The president and vice president earn $400,000 and $230,700 a year, respectively.

HEATHER

When I think of the women, men, and children I see every day at the hospital who can't afford the care they need, my heart truly breaks. But I know it's not just the families in my community who can't afford health insurance—it's a national problem that we have to address.

The scope of the problem Heather wants to address makes sense to solve at the federal level. Might a federal position make sense for you as well? You may think that you don't know enough to run for the House or the Senate, much less president. That you want to hold more local elected offices first. That's a fair point, but just a reminder: 45 *never held a political office in his life before becoming president.*

MEN. ARE. NOT. WAITING.

Of course, there are many things to consider (your career, the demands of the job, your and your family's relocation, the actual race). It is a big deal to run for federal office and will take an enormous amount of energy, time, consideration, and money. In just a few chapters we will figure out if this huge job fits into your life, but for now just write down whether or not the office might match the problems you've identified.

Are you into that DC life? _____

_____

_____

_____

_____

ONE OF THESE OFFICES IS WAITING FOR YOU

Some people spend years planning and strategizing where to run and when, and some people just wake up and decide they want to run for mayor. You can start local and work your way up. Or you could decide that you want to have a national impact on issues. And yes, first-time candidates win at the national level all the time.

Case in point: Alexandria Ocasio-Cortez was a political organizer and bartender before she ran for Congress. In her first campaign, she defeated Democratic incumbent Congressman Joe Crowley, who had not only been in office for twenty years, but was also the chair of the House Democratic Caucus (aka, he held the number-four leadership position among Democrats in Congress). If AOC can do it, then you can too!

When you think about your run for office, you could look at the issues you care about and match them to the office that most meets your goals (as we suggested previously). Or maybe an opportunity will present itself (for example, a member of Congress retiring, or the mayor stepping down) and you just go for it. There is no right way—there's only the way you're going to do it.

Based on what we've just presented, do you think you know where you want to run?

_____

_____

If you answered yes, then where? _____

_____

_____

If you aren't sure, what positions did you circle? _____

_____

_____

It's okay if you chose several offices or none. As we explore how running for a particular office will work in your life, you may come back to this chapter and change your mind. Hell, you may have already changed your mind. But whether you've pinpointed the office or are still wavering, no matter. Off to the next chapter you go.

KEEP READING. STAY WORKING.

We need you.

I'm Running for Office.

THE CHECKLIST

1. I know why it's IMPERATIVE that more women run for office. ❑

2. I was nominated by _____ .

3. Oh, hell yes, I'm qualified to run for office. ❑

4. I'm running for office to _____ .

5. **The office I'm running for is** _____ .

JUNE

KATE

> *Stacey Abrams keeps a list of her life's ambitions. Start your list here.*

She Believed She Could, SO SHE DID

Danica Roem

Search for "Danica Roem" on the Internet and you might find this headline: "What transgender legislator Danica Roem learned from Metallica." For the metalhead politicos out there, it's a great read. But it's not all you'll find on Danica. You'll also learn that she's the only openly transgender person elected to a US Statehouse.

In 2017, Virginia held its statewide and state legislative elections. In a mostly conservative Southern state with a few progressive pockets, Danica stood out with her notorious rainbow bandana. After working as a local newspaper reporter and editor for ten years in and around her hometown of Manassas, Virginia, Danica decided to run for state delegate in 2016.

She brought her journalistic roots to the campaign trail and looked at the issues from all sides—just as she had as a reporter. When her opponent, thirteen-term Republican incumbent state delegate Robert Marshall and his supporters made the campaign about Danica's gender identity, she reminded voters about the local issues they faced every day: traffic and congestion. On election night, Danica reiterated her promise of alleviating traffic on Route 28: "That's why I got in this race. Because I'm fed up with the frickin' road over in my hometown."

That's not all she said on her historic election night, though. Standing on a table in a local pub, Danica dedicated her win to (get ready to feel all the feels) "every person who's ever been singled out, who's ever been stigmatized, who's ever been the misfit, who's ever been the kid in the corner, who's ever needed someone to stand up for them when they didn't have a voice of their own. . . . This one is for you."

"**Tremendous amounts of talent are lost to our society just because that talent wears a skirt.**"

———FORMER CONGRESSWOMAN AND PRESIDENTIAL
CANDIDATE SHIRLEY CHISHOLM (D-NY)

Chapter Six

BUT THERE ARE SOME REQUIREMENTS, RIGHT?

Filing Deadlines, Age Limits,
Residency Requirements, Oh My!

★

Beth and Hilda Figure Out the Requirements
for the Offices They Are Interested In

Now that you have an idea of the position (or positions) you may want to run for (yay!), let's find out what the requirements are. There will likely be a minimum age and a residency requirement, and if you've been convicted of a crime, that could be an issue in some states.

There will probably also be **filing deadlines** to meet and fees to pay. Depending on the office, there may also be additional things you need to do. For instance, if you're running in a primary (where you will run against candidates from your own party to see who gets on the ballot for the general election) as an unaffiliated candidate (not tied to any major party), or as a write-in candidate, there may be different filing deadlines, signature requirements, or fees you'll need to know about.

 VERY IMPORTANT WORD ALERT **Filing deadline.** The filing deadline is the last day on which a candidate can file with the local, state, or federal elections board to run for office. This is the day by which all your paperwork must be completed and turned in.

Already know all the requirements for the position you're running for? Then skip to the next chapter, m'lady! If not, let's find out.

And when we say "let's," we really mean "you." It's on you to find out what seats are up for election, when the filing deadlines are, and what the specific requirements are. It's time to get a-googling! Need help getting started? Try searching these phrases:

★ "requirements for city council seat in XX city"

★ "elected positions in XX town"

★ "run for Congress in XX state or locality"

But before you do, let's see how Hilda and Beth figure out the basic requirements for the offices they want to run for.

HILDA'S (AFTER-SCHOOL) MARATHON

Hilda has some basic questions: what are the requirements for running for school board? Are there seats open? When are the filing deadlines?

I want to run for a seat on the school board. I'm trying to figure out exactly where to begin.

Here's how she gets her answers.

STEP ONE: Hilda googles "requirements for running for Los Angeles School Board."

STEP TWO: She clicks on the fourth result: "Run for Public Office—Los Angeles County."

STEP THREE: She clicks on "Election Candidate Handbook." And this is where things get overwhelming: Hilda sees a PDF of the 143-page candidate handbook, It's dense, daunting, and confusing.

STEP FOUR: Hilda sighs loudly. *This should be easier,* she thinks. Also, her two older kids are coming home in twenty minutes and her youngest is about to wake up from a nap. Once they descend upon the house it will be impossible to concentrate on anything.

The language in federal, state, and local candidate guidebooks varies and can be confusing. If you get overwhelmed while reading yours, find a lawyer friend to help you wade through the legalese. That way you can be sure you're meeting all the pertinent requirements and deadlines.

STEP FIVE: Hilda returns to the LA County webpage, the first page she was on. She sees a Contact tab. She clicks on it.

STEP SIX: Hilda calls the phone number listed. A nice woman gives Hilda another number to call at the LA County Registrar-Recorder's office. Hilda speaks to a woman there, and she forwards the call to the elections desk. The woman at the elections desk is helpful. HALLELUJAH! They have a convo that goes something like this:

Hilda: What are the requirements to run for school board in LA?

Helpful Lady: You have to be registered in the district.

Hilda: As a voter?

Helpful Lady: Yes.

Hilda: Is there an age requirement?

Helpful Lady: Not other than being old enough to register to vote. Here's a website you should go to.

The helpful lady gives Hilda a web address.

STEP SEVEN: Hilda glances at the clock. It's 2:47 p.m. She's got less than fifteen minutes before her kids come home from school and the insanity starts. She makes a mental note that her no-TV-until-after-bath rule will be relaxed for the day.

STEP EIGHT: Hilda goes to the web address that Helpful Lady gave her. She clicks on "Current and Upcoming Elections."

STEP NINE: She clicks on a link that says "Upcoming Elections."

STEP TEN: Hilda sees that the West Valley school board seat she wants to run for is currently open! She also sees kids from the neighborhood walking home from the bus stop—that means hers are not far behind. Hilda is sweating. She clicks on "Apply for Office."

STEP ELEVEN: She clicks on "Getting Started" and then on "Candidate Qualification and Filing Schedule."

STEP TWELVE: Hilda has found the goddamn info! She learns that the **nomination period** begins July 17 and ends August 11. It's only May! She has time! Yippppeee! Hilda does a little dance. Her children walk in and see their mom dancing alone to no music. They are concerned.

VERY IMPORTANT WORD ALERT The **nomination period** is the time period during which a woman needs to declare her candidacy and get all her paperwork in. These documents could include certification of her identity, address, proof that she is registered to vote, lists of signatures needed to obtain her place on the ballot, information regarding her campaign bank accounts and who her campaign treasurer is. The end of the nomination period is also the filing deadline.

So, in twelve not-so-easy steps, Hilda has her information. What now?

She needs to bookmark these websites so she can go back to them when she wants to refresh herself on the info. Details about **personal financial disclosures**, campaign finance regulations and information, and key dates are all things she's got to be able to access quickly.

Personal financial disclosure. When running for office or holding a public service occupation, it is not uncommon to have to report your personal financial information. This is meant to shine a light on any potential conflicts of interest that you, as a public servant, might have. Typically, the information you're asked to provide includes sources of income for yourself and your spouse; a range of annual income for yourself and your spouse; any investments you or your family may have; debts, including student loans, mortgages, car loans, and credit cards; any paid or unpaid positions held on boards, committees, or organizations; and any gifts or honoraria received over a certain value.

Now that she knows what the requirements are, that the seat is open, and when her papers need to be filed, Hilda is ready to go! She will figure out what people and organizations can help her with her campaign in upcoming chapters, but for now she has the key information she needs to get started.

IF YOU WORK FOR THE GOVERNMENT . . .

Federal government employees are generally prohibited from running for office and engaging in partisan political activity. Active members of the military can run for office, but they are prohibited from some necessary campaign activities—like raising money or soliciting votes—while on active duty. State and city governments have their own rules too.

Bottom line: if you work for local, state, or federal government or are currently in the military, research the Department of Defense directives on political activity, the Hatch Act, and your local laws on campaigning while working on behalf of American taxpayers.

SHAWNTA

Because I'm no longer on active duty with the military, I am cleared to run for political office. But I am going to check in with a friend who works at the Department of Defense to make sure there's nothing else I should know before I run on my military record.

BETH'S (WINE-SOAKED) JOURNEY

BETH

Now that I'm retired, I'm ready! I want to run for governor to fight for and protect all Iowan consumers. First things first, are there requirements?

You bet your ass there are, Beth.

Here is how Beth figures out what the requirements are.

STEP ONE: She fires up Lady Google, searches for "Iowa gubernatorial requirements," and finds the secretary of state's handy candidate guide. She opens the document and starts scrolling through.

STEP TWO: Beth pours herself a glass of wine. She finds the requirements for the governorship and thinks to herself:

❑ Must be a US citizen: *Check*

❑ Must be an Iowa resident for two years by the general election: *Check*

❑ Must be at least thirty years old at the time of the general election: *Oh honey, check*

STEP THREE: Beth sees a box that says "Signatures Needed." Okay, so how many signatures does she need? Beth takes a pretty big sip of wine.

STEP FOUR: Back to trusty Google. Beth searches "Iowa gubernatorial signatures" and finds another secretary of state page that includes "Signature Requirements—Senator and Governor." This tells her how many signatures she needs, the rules for collecting them, and how to file them with the state so she can get on that sweet, sweet ballot.

STEP FIVE: The answer? She has to collect thousands! 3,269 to be exact. And the signatures have to be collected from at least ten different Iowa counties.

Beth starts to do some mental math and tallies all her friends, her friends of friends, her friends of friends of friends. It doesn't add up to 3,269 signatures. She will have to put together teams of volunteers to collect those signatures. Beth pours another glass of wine. Takes another sip. This sip is actually a giant gulp. Beth is drunk.

But she has the info she needs and is aware that she will need a shit ton of volunteers to help her candidacy very soon. (For more on how to engage these volunteers, see Chapter Eight.)

It took Hilda twelve steps and Beth five steps and two glasses of wine to learn the requirements for their respective offices. Does it always take this amount of clicks, calls, and alcohol?

Well, it may. Or it could be as easy as showing up at a town meeting and having someone nominate you on the spot. Or someone could recruit you to run and have all the information at the ready for you. Or it could take you tons of phone calls and Google searches.

The moral of the story is that if you want to run for office and be a public servant, then guess what, sweet tits, ya gotta be willing to do the research to find out the basics. The information is there waiting for you—you just have to find it.

Head to ye olde Google, pick up the phone, and fill out the below:

What are the requirements for the position you want to run for? _____
_____

Do you meet them? _____

What information do you need to complete the paperwork for your candidacy? _____
_____
_____
_____
_____

How many signatures (if any) do you need to get on the ballot? _____
_____

When are the filing deadlines? _____
_____

GREAT, YOU HAVE THE BASICS DOWN.
KEEP READING. STAY WORKING.

We need you.

I'm Running for Office.

THE CHECKLIST

1. I know why it's IMPERATIVE that more women run for office. ❑

2. I was nominated by _____.

3. Oh, hell yes, I'm qualified to run for office. ❑

4. I'm running for office to _____.

5. The office I'm running for is _____.

6. **The filing deadlines for this office are** _____.

7. **The other requirements for this office are** _____.

8. **I have met those requirements.** ❑

JUNE

KATE

> *Need a reminder to make sure you're registered to vote? Write it here.*

She Believed She Could, SO SHE DID

Stephanie Murphy

Stephanie Murphy has been called many things: "The girl rescued at sea," national security specialist, professor, and most recently, congresswoman.

Born in Ho Chi Minh City, Stephanie fled Communist Vietnam with her family when she was just an infant. Her family joined others and set sail in small boats, hoping to cross the South China Sea to safer shores. But their boat ran out of fuel. Adrift and in open water, their fate seemed sealed. But then a US Navy ship came to their rescue with fuel and supplies and directed them to a refugee camp. From there, Stephanie and her family made their way to the United States and settled in Virginia.

When the 9/11 attacks occurred, Stephanie was working in the private sector as a strategy consultant at Deloitte. The attacks on the country that rescued her from the South China Sea called Stephanie to public service. She quit her job and went to work for the US Department of Defense.

Stephanie later moved to Florida with her husband to focus on business and raising their two children. She mentored young women and won an appointment to Rollins College as a business professor. Then, in 2016, the same passion and patriotism that lit a fire for Stephanie to enter public service was ignited again when the Democrat looking to challenge twelve-term Republican congressman John Mica dropped out of the race. Suddenly, an opportunity had presented itself. Stephanie had only six months to run a full-fledged campaign. She knocked on doors and got her message out, and it paid off. On election night, Stephanie won and became the first Vietnamese American woman to serve in Congress.

Stephanie's dedication to public service derives from her experience as a child being rescued by strangers at sea. She says, "My patriotism is the product of a life lesson, one instilled by US service members bestowing grace upon desperate strangers."

"No one asked me to run until I first made it clear that I wanted to . . . It's a great thing to recognize and name your goal, and there should be no shame in it."

—COLUMBUS CITY COUNCILWOMAN LIZ BROWN (D-OH)

WHEN DO I TELL PEOPLE I'M RUNNING FOR OFFICE?

SPOILER ALERT: THE ANSWER IS TODAY

Why Telling People
You Want to Run for Office Matters

★

Keeping Track of Who You Tell and
Taking in Their Feedback

Y ou've narrowed down what office solves the issues you care about and you've figured out what the requirements for that office are. How are you feeling about running now? Is the endeavor feeling more real and therefore so much damn scarier?

Or, conversely, are you feeling armed with tangible info and therefore more confident about moving forward?

Write a couple of sentences on how you're feeling about your candidacy right now.

Now, if you wrote that you are feeling good about taking this book out of your bag at the salon and working through it while you get foiled, that's rad. Keep reading and stay working. We need you.

If you wrote that you have pit sweats down to your waist and are wondering how you ever thought this could work . . . okay, girl. We hear you. What you're doing is huge. We sympathize with your anxieties, but here's the thing. Whether you feel energized and excited about your candidacy or scared out of your goddamn mind or a mixture of the two, no matter! It's time to take the next step.

It's time to announce.

Do we mean you need to stage a press conference and get on a podium and officially announce your candidacy? No, not yet. But we do mean you need to tell people you are thinking of running for office.

"But WAIT!" you may say. "I haven't finished the book yet! I'm only on page 74. I need to read and fill in all of the rest of the pages, and then I need to do some additional writing where I reflect on what I've learned, and then I need to call my best friend Zadie (I don't make a move in love or life without her) and let her know that in the next year or so (depending on the stars) I'll have an announcement." That might calm your nerves and feel great right now, but seriously, you can't wait that long. A reminder:

MEN. ARE. NOT. WAITING.

They are not waiting till they know more. They are not waiting till they've figured it all out. They are not waiting for the perfect time. So, let's not wait.

You're going to start announcing your plan to run for office. And you're going to do it ASAP.

Why now? Before you've finished this book? Because telling the people in your life that you are considering a run for office will accomplish two important things. It will . . .

1. LIGHT A FIRE UNDER YOUR OWN ASS. Saying something aloud makes that thing more real, doesn't it? Your words commit you; they hold you accountable. We are asking you to tell someone now because you are going to build a space for yourself where you can't wriggle out easily. You are going to account for your words and your promises. Just as you expect elected representatives to keep their promises, you're going to make one to yourself right now. Saying it aloud is the first commitment you are making to running for office.

2. LIGHT A FIRE UNDER THE ASSES OF YOUR FAMILY AND FRIENDS. Did you ever get hip to something before anyone else around you, be it an indie film, a Twitter feed, or a new podcast? Let your nearest and dearest be the first to get hip to your candidacy. If you engage them early and often, they will be the building blocks of your campaign. By telling your closest peeps (don't worry, you can start with just one) that you are thinking of running for office, you are bringing them along on your journey—right from the start. They will feel honored that you told them before anyone else. They will feel entrusted. They will feel connected to you. They will feel generous with their money, their time, their connections. These people will be the first supporters of your campaign. (Unless they have a bad reaction. More on that in a bit.)

If now seems awfully soon to start telling people (and saying out loud to yourself) that you want to run, remember . . .

MEN. ARE. NOT. WAITING.

Let's start telling the people closest to us.

Jordan Evans,
Charlton Public Library
Trustee

The first person I told I wanted to run for office was my mom. She has been there for me through every major life decision, every personal victory and heartbreak, and every dumb thing where I should've known better. I don't think she ever expected to have a daughter involved in politics, but that hasn't stopped her from doing her best to be as supportive and understanding as possible. Plus, other than being my biggest fan and closest consultant, she's a perfect source of blunt honesty about practically everything I do—including my campaigns!

Heads up: these are words we must say aloud and not text, email, or emoji. For example, **do not** send this text that Monika sent to her best friend, Kulap.

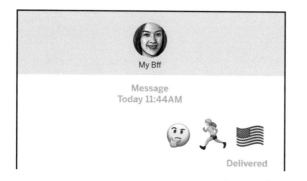

DO say this out loud: I am thinking of running for office.

Remember that elevator pitch you wrote on page 37? Use it to explain your reasons for running.

So, who ya gonna call? Write down the lucky folks who get to hear it first. _ _ _ _ _ _ _

_ _

_ _

When are you gonna tell them? _

_ _

_ _

Now do it! Come back when it's done.

Before we ask you how it went, we have to make sure you start an important practice of getting digits! It's essential that you write down the names, contact info, and feedback from the people you've told that you're running. You may be able to learn from any negative responses (more on that in a moment), and the positive feedback will be helpful to return to during the hard days when you may need to remind yourself just how supported you are.

These people will become your campaign Rolodex (aka contact list). Even if most of these people are people you know intimately and are among your top ten favorites on your phone, write them down. Continue to tell people you are running for office until your wider circle of coworkers, friends of friends, and acquaintances all know. Reminder: there will be more on how to engage them in Chapter Eight.

NAME	EMAIL	PHONE NUMBER	FEEDBACK
1			
2			
3			
4			
5			
6			
7			
8			
9			
10			
11			
12			
13			
14			
15			
16			
17			
18			
19			
20			
21			

How did the first announcement go?

❑ It went great!

❑ It wasn't great. I am more freaked out than I was before.

❑ Somewhere in between. I think it was okay, but I'm not sure.

Here's what happened when Heather told a coworker she was going to run.

HEATHER

I told Mai, my dear friend and fellow nurse, and it was a great experience. Before I could even get out the words "I want to run for office," she interrupted and asked if she could volunteer for my campaign. It was a proud moment at the nurses' station.

The reaction to Heather's news was super positive. Heather should *immediately* put Mai's name and her offer to help in the chart on the previous page, because she will soon be taking Mai up on this offer. If your feedback was just as positive with offers of help, make sure you *write these offers down.* We will be coming back to them.

And here's how it went for Monika.

MONIKA

I told my best friend, Kulap. She is a big part of my activist life and I thought for sure she would be supportive. It didn't go great. She seemed really surprised, and her first response was "Are you qualified? Don't you think you are too young? Don't you have to have a ton of money?" It was NOT the reaction I was hoping for. WTF? It made me wonder whether she's right—maybe I'm not qualified, maybe I am too young, and maybe I don't have enough money to do this.

First of all, oy. That's rough.

Second, Monika's experience brings up the important question of how to confront negative feedback. We have a couple of options. We can:

1. Believe the feedback entirely. Decide that we are not smart enough/rich enough/young enough/old enough to run for office. Think that Kulap is 100 percent right and that we are 100 percent wrong. Subsequently we can hide this book in a drawer, never to be looked at again, and implode in a cloud of self-doubt and self-hatred.

2. Dismiss the feedback entirely. Decide that we are 100 percent right and that Kulap is 100 percent wrong. Believe that Kulap is a giant dummy who has nothing to offer and beat ourselves up *only* for ever thinking that Kulap had a damn thing to offer us.

3. Listen to the feedback. Consider that voters may also have some negative assumptions about us and that this is a great opportunity to combat them. Monika could respond by saying, "I think having someone in office who understands the reality of living paycheck to paycheck is invaluable. I'm proud to give a voice to my age group and our specific concerns, and I'm working on a really exciting fundraising plan." (We will get to fundraising soon enough!) It's also okay if Monika doesn't say a word back to Kulap and just cries like a baby in front of her. The truth is, she now has an opportunity to try responding to negative feedback with positive responses.

We're liking Option 3. Learning to process feedback is crucial. What will come as a surprise to no one is that women candidates are subject to way more criticism than their male counterparts. It's important to be able to welcome constructive feedback and to learn from it, but it's also important to discern what feedback is not constructive and dismiss it entirely. You should feel empowered to dismiss any feedback that you find offensive, sexist, or racist or that diminishes your humanity, especially if it makes you feel physically, emotionally, or mentally unsafe.

GETTING COMFORTABLE WITH SELF-PROMOTION

By now you've said out loud that you are going to run for office! You've made the commitment to your friends and family and, most of all, to yourself. You don't have to have all the definitive answers on the "when" and "how" of this adventure. Those answers are coming shortly. But for now, just bask in the glow of having named it to claim it.

Oh, what's that? You haven't uttered a word about your run to a mortal soul? If this exercise is paralyzing you and making you doubt the process altogether, have no fear, we are here to help. Telling people you are going to run for office is the first of many, many, many, MANY times you will be talking about yourself to others (ideally in glowing terms) when you're campaigning. So it's time to get comfortable doing it.

For many women, self-promotion feels not just uncomfortable, it feels garish. Unseemly. Unfeminine, even.

But it wasn't always so. Let's go back to when you were just a babe. Remember when you brought your mom or dad a piece of lint you found on the carpet, toddling over to them to show them "Look, Mom! Look, Dad! It's a piece of lint! From our carpet! And I found it! IT'S ME! I'M THE GIRL WHO GOT THE LINT!" If you remember this younger version of yourself, you'll realize that you had no issues with self-promotion back then. You didn't wonder if showing off your lint was "polite." If it was your turn. Or if it might make someone else feel less than. You were a little girl simply presenting your awesome discoveries. Without apology. Without explanation. But with joy and enthusiasm! You need to harness that little girl.

Because here's the thing . . . .

You will be talking about yourself a lot—sharing your story, outlining your vision for how your community could be better, and bringing people into your campaign.

Pamila Jayapal,
Washington Congresswoman

Research shows that people simply don't listen to women's accomplishments. When they do, they often don't believe them. Reporters tend to gloss over them. So you just have to learn to tout yourself. Steel yourself to the cries of being overly "ambitious" or "confident." As I said on Twitter after a congressman tried to insult me and I called him on it and got him to apologize on the House floor, "Stand strong. Refuse to be patronized or minimized. Let the small guys out there be intimidated by you."

JUNE

Kate, can we retitle this book
"Let the small guys out there
be intimidated by you"???

KATE

No.

DEFINING SELF-PROMOTION

What do we mean by "self-promotion," exactly? Let's look at an example from our very own Kate.

Okay, let me try a little natural self-promotion in the course of our conversation. How are you, June?

KATE

I'm good, how are you? What have you been up to?

JUNE

Funny you should ask. I just went on a friend's radio show and talked about how we will elect more women into office. . . .

And that's how you self-promote!

KATE

JUNE

Excuse me, I need a minute.

KATE

WHY ARE YOU LAUGHING SO HARD? Yes, that is SELF-PROMOTION. You're very welcome.

JUNE

Kate, that is not an example we can use for Dear Reader. You are simply stating the facts and mentioning the thing you were involved in, but not uplifting YOURSELF or promoting your OWN amazingness.

KATE

Ugh, okay, maybe you're right. I had a hard time saying that, just so you know. And I was damn proud of it.

JUNE

I know you were, sweet girl.

Kate and June discuss and debate what Kate should have said. And Kate gives this more thought and attention than she has many of these chapters and then says the following:

KATE

June, I wanted to tell you something exciting. I'm super proud to be a leading voice on getting more women elected and I wanted to share my latest interview on SiriusXM's Signal Boost. I talk about how we can elect more progressive women to run up and down the ballot. I'm really proud of my appearance.

See the difference? It's about not just stating what you've done, but *uplifting* what you've done.

You can start with the people in your life who you know will be interested: those closest to you. The people who have been with you through good times and bad, and most likely have heard a LOT about your breakups, terrible professors or bosses, tough financial situations, and hormonal rages. These people truly *deserve* to hear about what's going well! Let's not rob these sweet people of that. Let's share!

So, to get started and to get comfortable with the idea of self-promotion, we've laid out a "self-promotion a day" goal for one week. Seven days of *one* piece of self-promotion a day. It can be as simple as dropping into a conversation that you just got a raise or telling someone you feel like you were a fucking great mom to your kids during a really tough home week. Put your wins out there.

One week is all we are asking for. And you have to share with a person. (Kate shared hers with June, a woman she had been writing this book with for months, and it was still hard.) Texts don't count. For now, you have to promote yourself with real humans and say the words aloud.

Here's how Heather, Beth, and Hilda did it.

HEATHER

I told some coworkers about a letter to the editor I had just written about how when the Violence Against Women Act (which included more protections for Native American women) came up for reauthorization in 2013, twenty-two male senators voted against it. My letter highlighted that we need to do more to protect women living on tribal lands from violence. To be honest, I didn't love this exercise. But I did it!

Because I was on television for so long as a broadcaster, I'm used to talking about my accomplishments, passions, and drive. For this exercise, at lunch with some friends, I casually mentioned that I had completed a marathon at age sixty-five! I told my girlfriends that I was really proud of how I trained and pushed myself. This was easy, but please don't make me ask them for money!

BETH

JUNE

Beth, we will address raising money shortly! Don't freak out!

At our PTA meeting this past week, I announced that I'd just been asked to coach the girls' volleyball team. Getting young girls off their phones and into athletics is really important to me, and I was totally honored to be asked. I felt very lame announcing it, but I gotta say, several women came up to me afterward to talk about it and congratulate me; it was very sweet. Many were surprised to learn that I was a Division I volleyball player in college. I didn't realize I had never mentioned that before!

HILDA

Now it's your turn. Start your one-week self-promotion exercise today. Who are the people you are thinking of sharing your awesomeness with? Let's do this. Now. What is one thing you are really happy that you accomplished? Got something in your head? Ok, pick up your phone and dial.

DAY	WHAT DID YOU SHARE?	WITH WHOM?
1		
2		
3		
4		
5		
6		
7		

Dare we ask . . . how did it go overall? _____

_____

Did it get easier as the days went on? _____

_____

Were people generally happy to hear about your success? _____

_____

These seven days were a small taste of what your average conversation, meeting, fundraising ask, interview, speech, social media posts, and campaign ads will be like when you're running for office. For some of you, this exercise might have been a breeze. For others it might have been a real struggle. But know that practice makes perfect. The more you self-promote, the more natural and the easier it will be. Soon enough you will have the confidence of the most mediocre of white men!

(Oh, and if you've come to the end of the week and haven't announced your plan to run for office, then head back to the beginning of this chapter, please!)

KEEP READING. STAY WORKING.

We need you.

I'm Running for Office.

THE CHECKLIST

1. I know why it's IMPERATIVE that more women run for office. ❑

2. I was nominated by _____.

3. Oh, hell yes, I'm qualified to run for office. ❑

4. I'm running for office to _____.

5. The office I'm running for is _____.

6. The filing deadlines for this office are _____.

7. The other requirements for this office are _____.

8. I have met those requirements. ❑

9. **I've told these lucky people I'm going to run for office, because making this promise to myself and others matters:** _____.

10. I've completed my week of self-promotion. ❑

> *Have some ideas for your campaign slogan? Put them here.*

JUNE

KATE

She Believed She Could,
SO SHE DID

Patty Murray

You can't do anything; you're just a mom in tennis shoes."

Those were the words that propelled Patty Murray into politics. They were spoken to her by a male lawmaker when Patty was protesting Washington State budget cuts on community colleges. As a teacher at a community college, she knew the impact of those cuts and wanted to make her voice heard in the debate. Patty was a mom of two children, an activist, and a teacher. She had served on her local school board and had been elected to the Washington State Senate when she decided to run for higher office.

When Patty ran for the Senate in 1992—the famous Year of the Woman—she rallied against "all the guys in gray suits and red ties" who were keeping women both like her and unlike her out of politics. She campaigned on issues that voters could relate to—better pay, family leave, and education. When she won, she declared: "Next January I'm going to take my tennis shoes back to the United States Senate."

Patty was the first woman to chair the Senate Committee on Veterans' Affairs and the first woman to chair the powerful Senate Budget Committee. She's fought to help women veterans access health care, make childcare more affordable, balance the federal budget, and ensure that no matter where a child lives, they have access to a quality education.

Turns out moms in tennis shoes can do pretty much anything they want to.

"*I couldn't have done it without the friends who dropped my kids off at school, who cooked them dinner, who took care of them when they were sick. Everyone got on board. My sister said, 'Oh, Blanca, we've been waiting for this.' And guess what? We won.*"

———

—CALIFORNIA STATE ASSEMBLY MEMBER
BLANCA RUBIO (D-CA)

Chapter Eight

WHO IS GOING TO HELP ME?

Who Are Your People?

★

How to Harness Your People
for Your Campaign

Remember that tattoo you thought was a great idea when you were sixteen years old? The two dolphins swimming around each other strategically located on your lower back, making it, in no uncertain terms, a "tramp stamp"? Who was with you when you got it? Was there a friend holding your hand? Talking you down a ledge as you turned green with pain and wondered aloud if one dolphin would suffice?

Who was the first person you called after you broke up with your last girlfriend/boyfriend/spouse? Who was by your side as you grieved? After you left a message on your ex's phone drunkenly slurring the words "I'm shining through," who told you that move wasn't weird AT ALL—that it was the most natural thing in the world and that indeed you *were* shining through (and your ex should know it!)? Who does a velociraptor impression that makes you laugh so hard you've had several bladder near-misses?

JUNE

Let's be honest with ourselves— some of them were misses.

Many of us turn to our family and best friends when we take on the big, scary things in life (illnesses, marriages, new jobs, divorces, child rearing, dolphin tattoos) and the little, fun things in life too (*Real Housewives of Every Major City,* nails, church choir). We rely on their support, guidance, nurture, and love.

There's no question that you'll be leaning on these same people when you run for office.

If you're on the other end of the spectrum and you're thinking to yourself, "Wait a sec—I don't have any people. Most of the day I'm alone. I'm slowly transitioning into a 'robe person,' and I'm almost certain one of my Precious Moments figurines started talking," that's okay. Some people like to be constantly surrounded by a gaggle of folks, others prefer to get together with one or two close friends, and still others enjoy spending time alone and online. That is OK. All of these people can run for office and win. You don't need to be a social butterfly to successfully run for office. But here is the deal: you *do* need a community of people around you. Large or small. You will need to reach out and connect with people to tell them who you are, why you're fired up and ready to go, and how they can be a part of it!

We are going to identify the people in your life who may help your campaign by:

★ Voting for you.

★ Supporting your life so that you can spend time campaigning.

★ Supporting you emotionally.

★ Volunteering for your campaign.

★ Joining your campaign team.

Running for office is not an individual sport—it's a team activity. Yes, you, the candidate, are the boss. It's your vision and your leadership that will propel your campaign to victory. But, you also can't do everything, know everything, or be everything all the time. You will need to build a team to help you succeed.

As you go through this chapter, we'll ask you to think about the people in your life and how they can help your campaign with everything from hosting events, coordinating volunteers, and designing a logo to stocking the office with snacks. If your campaign has a substantial budget and resources—we're looking at you, federal and statewide campaigns—most of these jobs will be filled by paid political professionals who have worked on numerous campaigns and have a depth of experience. But on smaller, more localized races, your friends, neighbors, the parents from your child's baseball team, and other volunteers will be giving you their time and expertise to meet these responsibilities.

As we identify the people in your life, think about how they can help your campaign, whether by voting for you, volunteering for you, assisting you (in a multitude of ways), or joining your campaign team. Consider their skills and professions in terms of how they can be harnessed to help your campaign.

WHO DO YOU NEED ON YOUR TEAM? (P.S. YOU MAY ALREADY KNOW THEM.)

Here are just a few of the positions found on most federal and statewide campaigns. Again, the extent of your team will depend on the size and budget of your campaign—local campaigns will be much smaller and likely rely heavily on volunteers, with only one or two paid staff members, if that. But even if you're running for an office in a tiny town, knowing about these positions can help you get organized and run an effective campaign.

★ **Campaign Manager:** This is your *person*. You will talk to them on the regular, and they will help execute your direction and manage the day-to-day operations of your campaign. You should like them, but above all, you should trust them to get the job done. They should be organized, detail-oriented, passionate about politics, a talented manager of time and people, and a good communicator. They should also be able to tell you what they think, not what you want to hear. You don't need a "yes" person for this job—you need someone who will tell it like it is, no matter if it's good news or bad, or whether they agree with you or not.

In a local race, your campaign manager is often a Jane of all trades. Because you won't have a dedicated staff member for each of the positions listed, as you would in a larger campaign, your local campaign manager will have to do a bit of all of these jobs.

★ **Finance Director:** Your finance director will help you and your team set a budget and create a plan to raise enough money to meet that budget. They may hire deputies or call-time managers to help you make fundraising calls, and they are there to ensure your campaign has the financial resources it needs to succeed. For a smaller campaign, think of whether you have a friend who is a great fundraiser for a charity she loves or someone who is great at handling money who could take on this role.

★ **Communications Director:** The communications director crafts the messaging strategy for the campaign. Working with you and your consultants, they will push your message to the media and voters each day. From handling tough questions from the press to drafting statements to speechwriting to managing other press staffers (if you have them), your communications director is your voice—use them and use them well!

★ **Research Director:** You are going to start your own research in Chapter Ten, but your research director will pick up where you left off. Their job is to know everything about you, your record, and your opponents. From votes to quotes and everything in between, your research director is the person who understands your vulnerabilities, but also knows your strengths and can help build a narrative that will win. If you don't have the resources to hire a researcher or consultant, task your favorite lawyer, librarian, or journalist friend with doing some digging on your behalf.

KATE

I don't have a favorite librarian. I'm gonna need to find one.

★ **Digital Director:** You will be your own digital director in Chapter Ten (and after that, if you can't pay one, ask a tech-savvy friend for some digital help). But bringing on a professional digital director will not only help you raise money online, but it will also ensure that when you are engaging with voters and supporters via the Internet, you're doing it in an intentional, direct, and strategic way. Moreover, as more campaigns are subject to hacking and attacks via the Internet, having a digital director who understands cybersecurity threats can be useful. As more and more voters look to interact and engage with politics online, digital directors are a must.

★ **Field Director:** Every campaign is decided by the voters. On Election Day, voters punch a ballot, touch a keypad, or write in a name indicating their choice of candidates. Hopefully they will be voting for you because you've knocked on their door, emailed them multiple times, and called them asking for their support, and they've seen your volunteers and campaign signs all over town. That's the work of your field director, the person responsible for understanding the voting population of your district, who your base of supporters are, and how to mobilize them to vote for you on Election Day. In a lot of ways, you can win or lose a race based on the competency of your field operation. For local campaigns that might not have the budget for a field director, think of the person who knows the community the best, and ask them to help divide the district into smaller sized areas. Using these smaller maps, you can locate every address and start knocking on every door in town.

★ **Compliance/Legal Advisor:** In every town, county, state, or federal election there are legal issues surrounding a campaign that you must know and understand. Whether it's knowing the reporting schedule and requirements for every donation you receive or checking your personal financial disclosure reports, having a compliance or legal advisor on retainer is a very good idea. Can you use the lawyer you used for your divorce/civil suit/arrest/professional work before? You can, but be mindful that they may not be versed in election law—which is what you really need.

★ **Human Resources/Operations Director:** Sometimes, because campaign budgets are tight and every dollar should be going to communicating with voters, money for human resources or operations is cut, especially on smaller or local races. But if you can afford it, we urge you to consider finding ways to professionalize your campaign. Even if your team is super small, your staff (and your campaign) will be better off with access to human resources professionals, who can help with issues like sexual harassment and unconscious bias training, health care, and retirement accounts.

JUNE

My dad worked out deals with the dentist who treated me and my sisters. I believe we agreed to pay him $10 a month for the rest of our lives. But look . . . we have great teeth. Actually, I had to get adult braces at the age of 23. Never mind.

★ **Consultants:** There are contract-based political professionals who are experts in specific areas like polling and data, creating online and television ads, printing mail and signs, fund raising, digital engagement, opposition research, and communications (just to name a few). For small and large campaigns, consultants can provide extra insight, expertise, knowledge, and strategic thinking. Although small races may not have the resources for a large team of consultants, bigger races tend to utilize their expertise. Don't be afraid to ask a potential consultant for their references. Afraid consultants are too expensive? Negotiate a contract and a payment schedule that meet your needs.

We told you that a campaign was a team effort! But don't let this list overwhelm you.

There are people in your life who are poised to help. You need them now way more than you did when you were getting that tattoo (the one you are now laser removing—in a cruel twist of fate, it's more painful to remove than to get!). Let's look at the people you already know, identify the people you might want to get to know, and help you turn these brunch-on-the-weekend friends into your get-out-the-vote friends. You will not run for office alone. It will take a village. And it will take *your* village, so let's find out who is in it.

YOU SAID I MIGHT KNOW THESE PEOPLE! WHO ARE THEY?

Let's begin by identifying your closest people: your best friends, family members, and confidants—people like June's friend who helped her insert her first tampon at age fourteen when she couldn't do it herself. To be fair, these people don't have to be *that* close. But they should be close enough to be in your Inner Circle.

IDENTIFY YOUR INNER CIRCLE

Look at your phone (come on, it's right next to you, it's not that hard). Who are the last ten people you texted? Who picks up your call at all hours? Who will be 100 percent honest with you, even when it hurts? Who drove your kids to school when your car broke down? These are your people, your official team—they are the folks you'll ask for money, support, advice, and time.

Sometimes this group is called your "kitchen cabinet."

"Kitchen cabinet" refers to your closest supporters and advisors. The term was created in 1831 when President Andrew Jackson fired his entire cabinet, except for the postmaster general. Instead, he turned to his unofficial advisors, which his opponents labeled his *"Kitchen Cabinet"* because of their *"backdoor"* access to the president.

Pramila Jayapal,
Washington Congresswoman

My husband is a big part of my inner circle. He is my partner, and he's a strategic campaigner himself. He has always been deeply involved in the political strategy and the day-to-day campaigning of my races, and he is there to comfort me on the invariable tough days of a campaign.

HOW TO GET YOUR INNER CIRCLE TO HELP YOUR CAMPAIGN

By now you have already told at least some of your inners you're thinking of running for office. (You did do that, didn't you? Don't make us ask you twice!) Was someone especially supportive? Did someone offer their garage as a campaign office or connect you with a politically savvy friend? You might ask certain members of this group to work for you, perhaps as an events coordinator or as a paid consultant, or maybe even as your campaign manager. You might ask them to volunteer for you or just to help you keep your most basic needs met while you're busy campaigning—maybe that's asking for help with housecleaning once a week, making sure the laundry is done and you have clean clothes for the campaign trail, or keeping as much Diet Coke in the campaign office fridge as is humanly possible.

Our point is this: you're going to ask these people for a ton of help.

When you ask them for help, be specific! Whether you're asking for help to make your campaign work in real life or for a contribution, the more specific you can be, the better. People are more likely to respond when you make a direct request.

Don't Do This:

BETH

> *Hi, neighbor of twenty years, can you help me with my campaign?*

Do This:

SHAWNTA

> *Work-wife Nikki, will you watch my daughter two nights a week?*

HILDA

> *Dear best friend and graphic designer Sara, will you design my campaign logo?*

MONIKA

> *Kulap, I'm still running for office and I need your help! Will you commit to putting up a hundred yard signs?*

HEATHER

> *Beloved sons, will you host and organize a young professionals' event for my campaign?*

Now write down the names and contact information of your Inner Circle and what you are going to ask of them.

NAME	EMAIL/PHONE	MY CAMPAIGN ASK
1		
2		
3		
4		
5		
6		
7		
8		
9		
10		
11		
12		
13		

IDENTIFY YOUR COMMUNITY CIRCLE

In addition to your Inner Circle, there are the people in your life whom you interact with but aren't tampon-inserting-close with. Nonetheless, they are certainly people you will want to engage on your campaign. Who knows, the friend you made campaigning for a recent ballot initiative might be an expert on web design and could build your campaign website. Or maybe that stylish friend of a friend you met at a dinner two weeks ago could help you pick out an election-ready wardrobe. Meet your Community Circle.

You'll want to keep in touch with them, update them, and engage them in your campaign. They could potentially be a part of your campaign team. These people could be:

★ Friends who aren't part of your Inner Circle

★ Neighbors

★ Members of organizations and clubs you're a part of

★ People you met while volunteering on other campaigns

* Members of your church, synagogue, or mosque, or other place of worship.

* Sorority sisters

* Former classmates and school friends

* Members of your alumni association

* Fellow PTA members

* People whose services you've used (for example, dog walkers, dry cleaners, hairdressers, lawyers, accountants, contractors, etc.)

* Union members

* Professional networks or associations

* Teammates on recreational sports leagues

* Members of your book or game clubs (Jane Austen, anyone? Bridge, anyone? D&D, anyone?)

* Coworkers (past and present)

* Extended family (even the cousins you don't talk to anymore)

Crisanta Duran, Former Colorado Speaker of the House

I knew that deciding to run for office was going to be a sacrifice and that I'd need help. I'd seen other leaders in politics and the community utilize the people around them. So, when I first decided to go down this path, I knew it was really important for me to have a strong support system around me.

Fill in the blanks. There are a million places where you connect with people for a million different reasons. Write in the names of the people you know and how they might be able to help.

NAME	HOW I KNOW THEM	EMAIL/PHONE	MY CAMPAIGN ASK
1			
2			
3			
4			
5			
6			
7			
8			
9			
10			

GROWING YOUR COMMUNITY CIRCLE

If you realize you have a dream Inner Circle but maybe not so many in your Community Circle, that's okay. Lots of us don't have hobbies that involve other people and aren't involved with a lot of organizations or clubs. We would prefer to have dinner with the same two ladies every Friday night at the same restaurant, ordering the same thing and eating at the same table because we think it's truly hilarious. If this sounds like you, then listen up and listen up good: It's time to get out of your comfort zone. You are going to need more people than Allison and Arusha, lovely as they are.

You need a bevy of supporters around you. Here's how you can get them.

1. JOIN JOIN JOIN. Are there groups that look hella awesome but you've never thought of joining (e.g., Crochet and Rosé at the Senior Center)? Or you've never had the time to? The moment has come to put on your bowling shoes and show up and *be with people.* Join in, make friends, tell them you're considering a run for office. AND GET EVERYONE'S CONTACT INFORMATION.

2. CONNECT CONNECT CONNECT. Tell people about your campaign and that you're looking for help/support/advice. You may know people who are connected to local politicians, unions, operatives, or activists. They may have run for office themselves or may have worked on a campaign before! Ask to be connected with *their* people. AND GET EVERYONE'S CONTACT INFORMATION.

3. SHOW UP SHOW UP SHOW UP. Did you recently get an email from Terra asking you to attend the neighborhood watch meeting? Did you delete it right away because you are slammed right now? That's fair, but you will need Terra to show up at the voting booth pretty soon. Consider showing up for Terra if you're going to ask her to show up for you. AND GET EVERYONE'S CONTACT INFORMATION.

4. HOST HOST HOST. Gather some friends for book club, a dance party, or a *90-Day Fiancé* viewing party. (Don't forget to start with *Before the 90 Days,* which is essential viewing.) If you know only Allison and Arusha, then invite them and ask them to each bring two of their friends. If you don't have the space to host, ask a friend if you can host an event at their place, or find a bar or restaurant where you can gather people together. AND GET EVERYONE'S CONTACT INFORMATION.

**Jenny Durkan,
Mayor of Seattle**

My advice? Start joining. Show up in your community and participate in organizations, causes, and nonprofits that are important to you.

5. BEFRIEND YOUR FRIENDS' FRIENDS. Check out your Inner Circle list. Circle people who have friends that you'd like to engage in your campaign. Don't be afraid to say to your people, "Are there people you think I should know?" Chances are you may have a lot in common with your best friends' friends and they could be natural supporters. AND GET EVERYONE'S CONTACT INFORMATION.

6. DON'T BE A DICK! As you move forward in your run for office, you are going to need people's support. Their money for the campaign. Their time to pick up your children or drop off a casserole. Their living rooms for fundraisers. When they help you with their money, time, and talent, thank them!

KATE

A handwritten card with a specific acknowledgment goes a long way!

Notice how throughout this section we encouraged you to GET EVERYONE'S CONTACT INFORMATION? By collecting business cards, phone numbers, and emails, you're building your list of future supporters. That way, when your campaign kicks off, you already have a go-to list of family, friends, allies, and *voters* you can rely on.

So start a Google Sheet or Excel file today. Title it, you guessed it: Campaign Supporter List. Transfer over the contact information you already gathered in this chapter. The goal is to grow the document. From now on, you need to get contact information for everyone you meet and talk to about running for office. That info needs to go into your spreadsheet.

HILDA

When I'm at volleyball games or school drop-off and I meet people and tell them I'm running, I immediately have my phone out and get their contact info. I've saved it all in a group called "Hilda for Office List."

Yes, Hilda, yes! Get phone numbers and email addresses and add them to your Campaign Supporter List! Save it and back it up. The folks on this list will be your primary followers as you're getting started. You'll reach out to them for money, guidance, and support. You'll send them holiday cards, invite them to events, ask them to coffee, tweet them updates, call and email them to ask for money and to volunteer! But right now you just need to get the digits.

KEEP READING. STAY WORKING.

We need you.

I'm Running for Office.

THE CHECKLIST

1. I know why it's IMPERATIVE that more women run for office. ❑

2. I was nominated by _____.

3. Oh, hell yes, I'm qualified to run for office. ❑

4. I'm running for office to _____.

5. The office I'm running for is _____.

6. The filing deadlines for this office are _____.

7. The other requirements for this office are _____.

8. I have met those requirements. ❑

9. I've told these lucky people I'm going to run for office, because making this promise to myself and others matters: _____

10. I've completed my week of self-promotion. ❑

11. **I've built my Campaign Supporter List in a good ol'-fashioned spreadsheet.** ❑

JUNE

Are there people you want to meet? List their names here.

KATE

She Believed She Could, SO SHE DID

Jenean Hampton

When Jenean Hampton's grade school classmates made fun of her for getting good grades, wearing glasses, or reading science fiction novels, she decided that instead of folding to peer pressure, maybe it was okay to "just be Jenean."

It's a mantra she's taken from where she was born and raised in Detroit, Michigan, to serving as the Republican lieutenant governor of Kentucky. When she was elected in 2015 and became the first African American ever elected statewide in Kentucky and the fourth woman to hold the title of lieutenant governor, she could still "just be Jenean." And it was that Jenean who spearheaded programs boosting entrepreneurship and initiatives dedicated to getting kids interested in math and science.

Watching her mother raise four children without a high school diploma, Jenean knew her family was struggling to get by. She committed herself to going to college and getting a well-paying job. She worked her way through college and then joined the air force and served for seven years, rising to the rank of captain. Her service included a deployment to Saudi Arabia during Operation Desert Storm, where she oversaw the use of radar used in search-and-rescue missions.

After her military service, she moved to Kentucky, worked for nineteen years in the private sector, and got involved in local politics. In 2014, she ran for state representative. She lost, but her campaign caught the eye of Kentucky political insiders. It wasn't long before gubernatorial candidate Matt Bevin tapped Jenean to be his running mate. When asked about the historical significance of her time in public office, Jenean downplays it, saying "I'm aware of the historic significance. I get that. A lot of people are excited about that. I'm probably more excited at the chance to encourage others, other nonpoliticians, to get into the game."

"I'm not asking for myself, I'm asking for the people of my district . . . And you have to ask specifically for money. Not just 'Help me however you can help me.' Instead, you say 'Can you give me $1,000?'"

———————

—CONGRESSWOMAN TERRI SEWELL (D-AL)

DO I NEED TO RAISE A SHIT TON OF MONEY?

Short Answer: Probably, but Size Matters

★

You Can Do It, We Can Help

Will you have to raise a shit ton of money for your campaign? The short answer is that you *will* need to ask for money, and you will most likely need to ask for money again, and then go back to ask for even more money. Before we dive into figuring out how much you will have to raise (and whether it's indeed a shit ton!), let's explore the relationship that women, as a demographic, have to money and the relationship *you* personally have with money. Not having access to money or access to people with money can be one of the biggest barriers of entry for women candidates. Let's read the bad news before we get to the really good news.

WOMEN AND RACE AND MEN AND WEALTH

As we've said before—and it bears repeating—more women are breadwinners than ever before, but we're still paid less than men. Moreover, women are 60 percent of minimum wage earners. At the same time that we are responsible for keeping our families financially secure, we are also getting paid less for doing the same work as men. And as of 2019, the federal minimum wage is $7.25 an hour and the federal tipped wage is $2.13 an hour. Yes, that's not a typo. $2.13 an hour.

And it's not just that we're paid less than men. Women have *accumulated* less wealth than men. Single women have just 32 cents for every $1 owned by single men. And for women of color, the wealth gap is even wider, with single African American women and Latinas having less than a cent for every dollar owned by single white men.

We do not, in general, have the same access to networks of wealth as men do. And we never have. How does all this grim info relate to your run for office? To put it simply: women need to reach out to the networks of people in their lives to ask them for money.

KATE

Remember the Campaign Supporter List you started in the last chapter? We're going to be asking those people for sweet hard cash pretty soon.

Compared to men, women are at a disadvantage. Men—read: white men—have been building their networks for centuries. They have bought, sold, and passed on property. They've helped each other build and secure wealth for their futures. They've assumed leadership roles in companies, organizations, and governments. In short, men have remained dominant by perpetuating modes and structures of power. Women, however, have not had the same access to inherited power or wealth. And for as long as our democracy has existed, access to power and wealth have been critical to seeking political office. Even men who simply kept up the appearance of power and wealth could get elected to office more easily than women. The political elite have viewed power and wealth as signs of a successful candidate, whether as a result of their ability to fundraise from their equally rich networks, their ability to self-fund their own campaigns, or their political strength in their communities. And when you don't have access to power and wealth? Fundraising can be more difficult, powerful donors and networks are not as open and available, and you're not seen as a viable candidate. Does this sound like it might affect any demographic we know? (Hint: it's women.)

The hurdles to leadership for women—stereotypes, biases, and barriers—are even higher for women of color. This is especially true in fundraising. Research shows that female candidates of color are more likely than white women to have a primary challenger—which means they need more money early in their campaigns. And as research from the Center for American Women and Politics at Rutgers University has found, "Black candidates often raise less money, rely more often on small donations, and are more likely to need to seek campaign donations from outside of their districts, which are less affluent—on average—than those of White candidates."

This is important information to digest if you are a woman of color. And also if you are a white woman. And if you are supporting a woman of color candidate, recognize that she needs more money . . . and donate it to her campaign now.

We don't want lack of access to wealth and money to stop you from running. Let's get to the good news about you and money. We promised there would be good news, after all! So let's start talking about your specific relationship to money, how much money you are going to need, how you are going to ask for money, and who you are going to ask for it from.

WE SAY MONEY, YOU SAY_____?

A LOOK AT YOUR SPECIFIC RELATIONSHIP TO MONEY AND A FORMAL INVITATION

Is there anyone among us who has a truly neutral relationship to the almighty dollar? Who couldn't care less if they have it or don't? For most of us, depending on the history of our finances, whether we grew up with it or without it, money can trigger a strong emotional response of shame, confidence, embarrassment, desire, elation, or desperation (or some mixture of all of the above). Unless the world changes dramatically, as a candidate, you will have to ask for money. That very first ask will be loads easier once you identify and explore your current relationship to money. Trust us. By first acknowledging any uneasy feelings about money here, you are helping to ensure that donors will hear a strong, confident voice asking for their support on the other end of the line. So, Dear Reader, what is your relationship to money? Check all that apply.

❑ I'm embarrassed that I have money.

❑ I'm embarrassed that I don't have money.

❑ I don't like to think about money.

❑ I'm uncomfortable asking for a raise.

❑ I'm proud of the salary I negotiated.

❑ I'm ashamed that I inherited wealth.

❑ I'm ashamed that I grew up in poverty.

❑ I'm proud that I grew up knowing the value of money.

Write your feelings about money here: _____

_____

_____

_____

_____

_____

If those feelings are all positive, then great! Move ahead, unicorn woman. If your feelings around money, however, are generally negative and riddled with shame, embarrassment, and greed, we are going to invite you to do something revolutionary. Truly something absolutely nuts-McGee.

Dear Reader,

You are formally invited to forget everything you've ever felt about money.

Sincerely,
June and Kate

Forget all your discomfort. Forget it all. Because you are starting a new relationship with sweet, sweet cash. You are now raising money to change the world.

Have you completely forgotten your old relationship with money? Great. Because you are now going to get comfortable with asking for money.

Campaigns in this country cost money, and candidates rely on donors to provide that cash. As a candidate in a larger race, a majority of your day will be focused on raising money—whether by making calls to donors or attending fundraising events. Even for a local or smaller office, a portion of your day or week will be devoted to raising money. And that doesn't stop once you're in office. Members of Congress spend at least half their day making calls, just to meet their fundraising goals. And, of course, there are donors, corporations, and political groups who use their financial giving power to access candidates and elected officials. While Congress and states have worked to curtail just how much money can go into campaigns and politics, it is still hard to separate money from our over-two-hundred-year-old political system.

However, there is progress: Democrats, helmed by Speaker of the House Nancy Pelosi, have proposed to reform our campaign finance system by introducing a small-dollar public matching system. The idea is to entice candidates away from spending so much time and energy focused on wealthy donors and instead redirect them to focus on small-dollar donors, so they could receive a six-to-one match. Not a bad idea. Moreover, several elected officials, including Senators (and 2020 presidential candidates!) Elizabeth Warren, Kamala Harris, Amy Klobuchar, and Kirsten Gillibrand, have refused to accept corporate PAC donations to their future campaigns.

Some states and cities have made important strides in campaign finance reform. As of this book's publication, fourteen states have some sort of public financing campaign system. Thirty-nine states limit the amount of money an individual can give. And cities like Portland and Baltimore are proposing initiatives that would help local candidates match small-dollar donations with public dollars. And to get *even more* people engaged in local elections, some cities, like Seattle, Austin, and Albuquerque, are interested in "democracy vouchers," where eligible voters are given a set amount of money to donate to the candidate of their choice.

WHAT WILL I BE DOING WITH THIS MONEY?

To put it simply: the more money you have, the more people you can talk to about why you're running. The more people you talk to, the more voters you win. It will vary from campaign to campaign, but the money you raise might be spent on:

★ Paying for staff, organizers, and consultants

★ Building and maintaining your website

★ Shooting TV ads and buying airtime

★ Online content and communications

★ Printing direct mail and flyers

★ Polling or data

★ Renting office space

★ Making campaign swag (T-shirts/buttons/flyers/stickers/lawn signs)

HOW MUCH MONEY WILL I NEED TO RAISE TO DO ALL THAT?

Of course, different campaigns cost different amounts. There is no set amount of money, no universal goal or budget, that you will have to raise for every race.

So how do we figure out exactly how much *you* need to raise for your race? There are several questions to ask to help you narrow down a goal.

KATE

Remember you will **raise** this money—you don't have to have it in your personal checking account or have a rich uncle (though that never hurts).

★ Is yours a federal, statewide, or local election?

★ How much have previous candidates running for your office raised?

★ Is public financing available?

★ Do you live in a big media market, like New York or Boston, where it can be expensive to buy ad time on TV or the radio?

★ Do you have a large online network you can mobilize to raise money?

★ Are there limits on how much people can donate? If a donor can give only $100 for your race, you will have to spend more time asking many more donors to give to your campaign to meet your goal.

OTHER FACTORS TO CONSIDER

When it comes to election fundraising . . . size matters. For example in 2016 it cost, on average, $12.2 million to win an **open seat** in the Senate. At the same time, it cost *only* an average of $1.6 million to win an open seat in the House. That's a $10.6 million difference. A statewide federal race costs way more than a congressional district race. And fundraising for state races can vary from state to state, sometimes because of the size of the state. Bigger states mean more ground to cover and more voters to connect with. In 2014, the incumbent governor of Vermont spent $961,469 to win reelection. In the same year in Texas, a gubernatorial candidate for an open seat spent $40 million to win.

VERY IMPORTANT WORD ALERT An **open seat** means there is no sitting incumbent seeking reelection.

Limits on how much people can donate matter. As of 2019, the federal government allows individuals to give $2,800 to candidates per election (once in the primary and once in the general election). And each state regulates how much individuals can give to candidates running for governor, the state legislature, and local offices. For example, as of 2018, in Maine, individuals can give a maximum of $1,600 to gubernatorial candidates and $400 to state legislative candidates, while in California, individuals can give $29,200 to gubernatorial candidates and $4,400 to state legislative candidates. And as of the time we're writing this, in eleven states (Alabama, Indiana, Iowa, Mississippi, Nebraska, North Dakota, Oregon, Pennsylvania, Texas, Utah, and Virginia) an individual can give *unlimited* amounts of money to candidates.

Challenging a sitting officeholder or incumbent matters. It will likely (though not always) cost more to challenge a sitting officeholder, or incumbent, because you will need to spend money on television, radio, and online ads, as well as mailings, emails, and other forms of communication, to introduce yourself to your community and tell them why they should vote for you. The current officeholder has a slight advantage because their constituents—for better or worse—already know who they are and what they are about. For example, in 2016, an incumbent House candidate raised and spent an average of $2.2 million to win their competitive race. In the same election cycle, it cost a House challenger an average of $2.7 million to beat the incumbent.

The same questions we asked previously about the size of the community you're looking to represent and incumbency versus challenger status should be asked about local races too. For example, an incumbent running for reelection to the school board in Minneapolis, Minnesota, raised approximately $40,000 for her campaign. Her challengers raised between $180,000 and $220,000. Usually, incumbents have already established themselves with donors, voters, and the community they represent. They've been raising money at a steady clip since they've been elected, so they most likely have a sizable bank account to rely on already. Unless they have a particularly hard or difficult challenger running against them, they might not have to spend as much, because they've already built up their name identification and reputation with voters. All of that can make it difficult for challenger candidates to unseat them.

Learning from other campaigns matters. Every campaign is unique, from the political environment and the candidates to the issues at hand. No one else has run your campaign before. But there are strategies that have worked in the past, and these strategies can impact how much money you raise. Do some research, go online, read old newspaper stories about past elections for the seat you're looking at.

Trust and believe, women have done a lot to raise money. Some candidates have put their personal financial futures on the line to run. Congresswoman Nanette Barragan (D-CA) took out a home equity loan on her house to pay for her campaign. Other women have taken personal loans to finance their campaigns. When Barbara Mikulski, the former Democratic Maryland senator and the longest-serving woman in Congress, first ran for office, she held "Bingo for Barb" and "Bowling for Barb" fundraisers.

There are ways to fundraise that don't include bingo and bowling, love those activities as we do. Consider online crowdfunding campaigns. Social media is a great way to raise awareness of your campaign and to bring in small-dollar donors. Entice donors to donate by entering a contest to win a prize—lunch with the candidate, prime seating at an election night party, or a spot on your Fourth of July parade float! And if you have the money, T-shirts, buttons, and stickers never hurt. NPR wouldn't give you that tote bag if they didn't think you'd give them a $25 donation. Swag works.

Be mindful of the political climate you're running in. Has the opposing party held the seat you're looking at for decades? Your campaign might just be the right inspiration for your party's donors, who are looking for a fresh face (like yours!) to lead. Do political experts report that voter support for the incumbent might be slipping? That could be a helpful talking point in your fundraising pitches. What are the issues that other candidates running for your seat in the past have focused on? Are national events like a presidential election happening at the same time as yours? Bigger elections might impact your campaign in terms of donors getting asked by more candidates to give money.

The amount of money previous candidates have raised matters. Research how much previous candidates had to raise to run their campaigns. That number will signal what someone else thought was a reasonable amount to raise for that particular race to pay for his/her candidacy. A precedent was set and should be considered (but not necessarily met).

How do you find out how much money the last candidate in the seat you're running for raised? General rule of thumb: For federal races, the Federal Election Commission and OpenSecrets.org are great free resources. For state and local, try the state or local elections board or FollowTheMoney.com.

Do you need to spend the same amount as your opponent or the incumbent to win? Not always. In 2018, a former math teacher named Mary Wilson won the most votes in the Democratic primary election for Texas's Twenty-First Congressional District. She raised $40,000. The closest runner-up? He raised $770,000. The money she raised covered her transportation costs to travel around her district. Mary's story reminds us that sometimes you just need enough money to get from campaign stop to campaign stop.

You don't necessarily have to raise the same amount as your opponent, but knowing how much money they have is important. You will use that number as a barometer to help you figure out how engaged the community is in your opponent and in your race. If your opponent has raised a lot of money over the years from a lot of local donors, that shows that he or she has a strong base of support who is ready and willing to donate every time they're asked. But if your opponent doesn't have a lot of money, that might suggest they are vulnerable to a challenge and do not have a deep bench of committed donors or supporters.

Ayanna Pressley, Massachusetts Congresswoman

In order to provide for my family and to make ends meet, I made the decision (like many of my fellow women colleagues in government or running for office) to cash out my 401(k). It was a sacrifice and a big gamble—one that fortunately paid off, but also one I wouldn't recommend.

FIGURING OUT MY FUNDRAISING GOAL

Let's look at how some of our candidates figured out the amount of money they needed to raise to win. **Heather's** running for Congress in North Dakota.

HEATHER

So in 2018, the current congressman raised $1.8 million, and he spent $1.2 million of that on his last campaign. His opponent raised $306,000 and spent $299,766. The congressman won by 46 points.

Heather, how did you find these numbers?

HEATHER

I went to OpenSecrets.org, which tracks federal campaign contributions.

Thanks, Heather.

Here's what Heather discovered at OpenSecrets about the last election for her congressional seat:

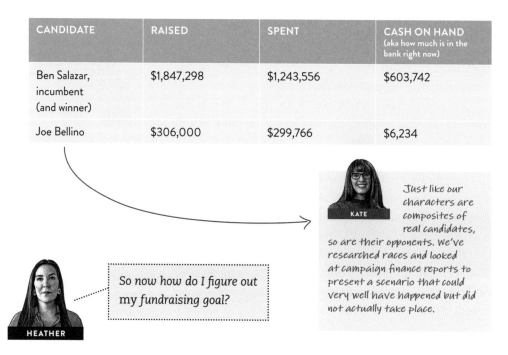

CANDIDATE	RAISED	SPENT	CASH ON HAND (aka how much is in the bank right now)
Ben Salazar, incumbent (and winner)	$1,847,298	$1,243,556	$603,742
Joe Bellino	$306,000	$299,766	$6,234

KATE

Just like our characters are composites of real candidates, so are their opponents. We've researched races and looked at campaign finance reports to present a scenario that could very well have happened but did not actually take place.

So now how do I figure out my fundraising goal?

HEATHER

Okay, Heather, let's consider the facts.

1. Heather is a first-time candidate without name recognition. She will need money to get her name and ideas out there.

2. The incumbent has been in office since 2004 and has been raising money since then. Also, everyone knows who he is, and likely has an opinion about him—which could be good or bad.

3. Heather knows that her opponent has $600,000 in the bank.

4. Heather is not personally wealthy and doesn't have access to wealthy donors. However, she has her union's support and the likelihood of its endorsement. That may not be direct financial support, but it will be meaningful. She also knows a community of activists from her work protesting the Dakota Access Pipeline. She might be able to tap into the large grassroots networks of the Standing Rock Sioux Tribe and national support from those involved with the protest to raise money online and grow her base of support.

5. Heather is running for Congress in North Dakota, which is an At-Large district—meaning it covers the entire state. She might need more money for transportation, offices, and staff because her district is so big.

HEATHER

Considering all of those facts, I would like to try to raise at least as much money as the incumbent did in his last race. My fundraising goal is $1.8 million.

Heather is an unknown, first-time candidate, so raising this much money might be a challenge. But to get her story and message to North Dakota voters, she will need the money to compete with her opponent. To raise it, she can get help from national organizations dedicated to electing women like her (more on this in Chapter Fourteen), engage her own progressive networks, and leverage her connections to large online activist communities.

There you have it. Thank you, Heather. Now let's hear about how **Shawnta** determined her fundraising goal for her run for Virginia Beach City Council.

SHAWNTA

The incumbent has held the seat since the eighties. I looked at the Virginia Public Access Project, which reports local campaign finance information in Virginia, and found out he spent $25,250 on his last election.

Shawnta is considering the following facts to come up with her fundraising goal:

1. She's well-known in her community for her nonprofit work helping veterans.

2. Because of her nonprofit, Shawnta has a lot of experience raising money and meeting her goals.

3. She has a large network she can reach out to, including groups dedicated to electing more veterans, like her, to office.

4. Her city council seat is currently held by a long-time incumbent with a significant presence in the community.

SHAWNTA

So, based on the success I've had raising money for my nonprofit, I feel pretty confident I can raise the $40,000 I need for my campaign. If I don't spend it all, I can save it for my next race.

That sounds like an awesome idea. And now on to **Beth**, who's running for governor of Iowa.

It was a little tricky to figure this out. The current governor isn't running again. The lieutenant governor is running to replace him. In their last campaign, they raised $5 million. GASP!

How did you find that number, Beth?

The trusty Internet! I found an article from the Des Moines Register that reported the fundraising totals from the last campaign.

Beth does some more research and finds that her opponent, the current lieutenant governor, has already raised $4.2 million. And she sees that other Democratic candidates running in the primary have raised between $299,000 and over $3 million. The money race is clearly on.

I know campaigns are expensive, but $5 million is more money than most Iowa families ever see. This money could be better spent going to services that Iowans desperately need—I have a problem with this!

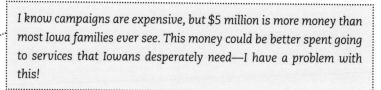

Beth, we hear you, we hear you! As governor, tackling campaign finance reform—at least in Iowa—could be a top priority for you! And here's another way to think about the money: the millions of dollars you raise for your campaign will go toward services that Iowans need—your services, your vision, your passion, your ideas.

How does Beth figure out her fundraising goal? Beth is considering these facts:

1. The previously elected governor spent almost all of the $5 million he raised in his last campaign, which means this could be an expensive race.

2. Beth will need a lot of money to campaign across the entire state. She'll need offices in big cities and some of the small towns. She'll also have to travel extensively through Iowa's ninety-nine counties. Beth will need a large campaign team to maintain and staff several offices across the state.

3. Before Beth can take on the incumbent, she's got to win a primary against several other Democratic candidates. So she needs early money to win the primary.

4. The fact that Beth's opponent, the lieutenant governor, hasn't had to run on her own before could help level the playing field for Beth. Voters will have the option of voting for both women for the first time.

5. Beth is well-known, well-liked, and trusted due to her many years as a TV news reporter. She also has a deep network in- and outside Iowa that she can tap into.

What is her fundraising goal? To get some guidance on this decision, Beth reaches out to Jess, an Iowa political consultant she once interviewed for a campaign story. After talking to Jess over several cups of coffee and hearing more about the cost of staff and travel, the ideal size of her budget for TV, radio, and online ads, and the cost of the last governor's race, Beth makes a decision. She will raise at least 70 percent of what the previously elected governor raised—$3.5 million. But she plans to raise at least half of that for the primary election. She needs this large sum of money early in her campaign to compete in the crowded Democratic primary field. She's going to be facing multiple candidates, some who can self-finance their own campaigns. She can't afford to sit back and raise the money slowly over time. If she wants to face off against the Republican nominee in November, she's got to have the money and a strong campaign ready to win the primary election first.

LET'S FIGURE OUT YOUR FUNDRAISING GOAL

Now it's your turn. Please fill in the answers below.

What position are you running for? _____

How much money did the previous winning candidate raise? _____

What are the factors that will impact how much you need to raise (name recognition, size and scope of the seat you're running for, status of incumbent/candidate, access to endorsements, networks, donors)? _____
_____
_____
_____

What is your fundraising goal? _____

If you are totally overwhelmed by how much to raise based on how much past candidates in the same office have raised and if you don't know a single person to consult, do not panic. Wait until we tell you about how many groups you can contact for guidance on this subject in Chapter Fourteen: THE HOLY BIBLE. But for now, let's talk about how you are going to get dat money. We'll start by figuring out who is going to give it to you.

WHO IS GIVING ME THIS MONEY?

You do not have to be rich, nor do you have to have rich friends, to run for office.

Would being rich or having rich friends make your run so much easier? Maybe. But maybe not. If you are personally very wealthy, you have to be wary of having made investments that could be seen as problematic and also of having any conflicts of interest that could impact your campaign. Then again, possible conflicts of interest, problematic wealthy friends, and a ton of legal issues could all turn out fine and you could end up being president. Sound like anyone we know?

On the other hand, not having access to wealth can be a part of your personal story that many people will be able to relate to. Voters may welcome someone who has shared their struggles to pay bills and make ends meet. In 2018, 244 candidates for Congress had personal debt. More than 60 percent of the candidates in competitive races reported some kind of liability. For example, Lizzie Pannill Fletcher in Texas reported over $30,000 for a car loan. Susie Lee in Nevada reported holding over $25,000 in credit card debt. And Lucy McBath in Georgia had more than $10,000 in debt. But that didn't stop any of these women from running . . . or winning.

So the people and networks around you don't have to have money. You will, however, have to ask them for money. You will start by asking your Inner Circle and your Community Circle to give you money.

But to answer your question "Who is going to give me this money?" The answer is everyone you know and everyone they know and

JUNE

We will be addressing your Online Circle soon enough. We would never forget about the nameless strangers who follow you on your social media platforms.

then, depending on the size of your race, many, many, many people you don't know. Even if you're running in the smallest race at the most local level, chances are you will need to raise money from people you don't know.

HOW DO I ASK FOR MONEY?

No matter if you're running for president of the United States or for your local town council, fundraising will take up some of your time. It takes hours of making phone calls to people—some you may know, and others will be complete strangers. It is literally called **"call time."**

VERY IMPORTANT WORD ALERT | **Call time** is the scheduled time during which you will make fundraising calls. You will have a number of call-time hours scheduled each week. The number of hours is based on how much money you need to raise.

You will want to skip it. You will want to schedule yourself out of it. Resist that urge. This time is sacred. Failing to put in the hours to make the calls you need could mean the difference between winning and losing. So pick a comfy call-time chair. Be one with the chair. As mentioned earlier, you will spend time building your donor lists from the people on your Campaign Supporter List. You will call people on those donor lists and ask them for money. And then you'll call more people—people who have donated money to other campaigns like yours, people who generally give to candidates in your political party, people who've given to candidates with a profile similar to yours, and people who don't like your opponent.

Outside of making calls, you can raise money online with email blasts, online ads, via your website, through social media, and with in-person events. You will ask for money at breakfasts, lunches, happy hours, and dinners. The Internet allows you to reach voters all over the country and make a case for why they should help you run and win. But at the end of the day, you will still have to use your voice and ask for money.

Crisanta Duran,
Former Colorado State
Speaker of the House

I've found the most effective way to ask for money is to make it about your vision, not about you. Focus on what you want to accomplish. Lead with your ideas and values for the position you're running for. It's easier—and more effective—than asking, "Hey, can you contribute money to me and my campaign?"

HILDA

But asking for money makes me deeply uncomfortable! WHAT DO I SAY?

Here are some pro tips to get you started.

★ **First, are you sitting up?** Shoulders back. Head high, chin raised. Take a breath. Confidence matters here. If you feel awesome, it will be conveyed, even through the phone line.

★ **Next, let's change the entire framing of this conversation.** You aren't *asking* for money, you are *offering* someone an opportunity to participate in changing the world. You are passionate and care about your community and have concrete, actionable ideas on how to make it better. You're not walking around peddling slap bracelets from the early nineties. Wait . . . are you?

Remember your pitch from page 43? Copy it here: _____
_____
_____
_____
_____

Now add a line asking for a donation. You need to make a **hard ask** for a specific amount.

VERY IMPORTANT WORD ALERT A **hard ask** is when you ask for a specific amount of money from a potential donor. It's no-holds-barred, direct, and unapologetic.

Here are a few examples of hard asks:

"You've heard my vision for our community. Now I'd like to invite you to be a part of this campaign. Can I count on you to join us and contribute $1,000?"

"I am the leader we need to create real change for our community. I'm reaching out to a select group of individuals like yourself to invest in our campaign early. Can I count on you to contribute $1,000 to help make this campaign successful?"

Add your ask to your pitch below: _____
_____
_____
_____
_____
_____

Time to *practice*! Seriously, practice, practice, practice. Say your pitch and ask out loud. You don't want the first time you're saying it to be when you're asking for money or support. In fact, you should start with a trusted friend who can tell you how it comes off. Here are a few other tips to consider as you're practicing:

★ **After you make the ask, stop talking.** Let them respond. If you feel like you want to fill the silence, don't! Take a sip of water. Bite down on your pencil. Imagine that whoever talks first, loses. Get comfortable with discomfort. Sometimes, to fill any awkward or long pauses, we can try to fill in the gaps with unnecessary justifications, apologies, or more explanation than is necessary. Instead of giving someone a reason to say no, do whatever you can to wait for the person to respond.

★ **Remember that you are not personally asking for money.** You are asking for money on behalf of the change you want to make. On behalf of the causes you believe in. This is not about you.

★ **If someone says yes, that's great!** Thank them and end the call letting them know you'll be back in touch with future campaign updates (aka asking them for money again). **If someone says no, it's not the end of the world.** Again, this is not about you! Follow up and see if they can donate a smaller amount. If that doesn't work, consider asking them to volunteer.

Monika practiced with her girlfriend, Patrizia. Here's how the practice call went.

MONIKA: Hi, how are you? My name is Monika Alvarez. How are you? I wonder if I could have a moment of your time? I'm running for city council.

PATRIZIA: Uh, hi. I can't really talk right now.

MONIKA: I understand. Sorry for bothering you. I just wanted to call to maybe ask if you'd donate to my campaign.

PATRIZIA: No. I'm not very political and I don't have money to give you.

MONIKA: Okay, thanks. Sorry to bother you. Goodbye.

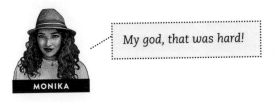

My god, that was hard!

MONIKA

Monika, thank you for being our guinea pig. And yes, this can be very hard. Here are a few things Monika should have done:

1. Monika should have given her pitch in the first sentence of the call.

2. She should have asked for a specific amount. A specific amount tells the donor you know what you need. It also acts as a starting point for negotiating a contribution. For example, if Monika asks for $250, Patrizia might say no, but Monika could follow up and ask for $150 or $125. If Monika asks for a contribution without a specific amount, and gets turned down, there's no negotiating from there—it's just a simple no.

3. Monika apologized twice and said she "*just*" wanted to ask for money. She used language that didn't invite Patrizia to be a part of her team by contributing and made her candidacy seem like an imposition on Patrizia's day. Instead, Monika should consider this call the best thing that will happen to Patrizia ALL DAMN DAY. Fortunately, Monika tried again!

> **MONIKA:** Hello, my name is Monika Alvarez and I'm running for city council to ensure that immigrant families are not only protected but represented in our government. As a first-generation immigrant, I know firsthand what the needs of this community are. I plan to be their voice in office. I'd like to invite you to help me make this vision a reality. Will you invest $250 in my campaign?
>
> **PATRIZIA:** Thanks for the call, Monika. I agree that we need more voices like yours in office. I don't think I can do $250.
>
> **MONIKA:** I understand, Patrizia. I know that you and I agree that our city needs new leadership who understands how we can make sure all families get a fair shot at success. But I need your investment to ensure I can share my vision with all of the voters we need to win. Can you consider $150?
>
> **PATRIZIA:** I can do $150.
>
> **MONIKA:** Thank you! My colleague Sara will follow up to collect your pledge. I look forward to updating you throughout the campaign on how we're doing!

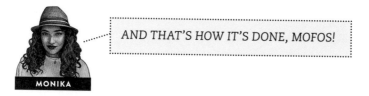

MONIKA

AND THAT'S HOW IT'S DONE, MOFOS!

Monika has every reason to be happy. She is now $150 closer to her fundraising goal. A few things to note about this second try:

1. Monika landed her pitch. It was short, to the point, and at the beginning of the call.

2. She invited Patrizia to be a part of the campaign—she didn't apologize.

3. She listened to Patrizia. She understood her concerns and mirrored her responses to meet Patrizia in the conversation.

4. She didn't give up when Patrizia said no the first time. Monika negotiated her ask and came away with a contribution.

5. She handed off the phone to Sara. To maximize the number of people Monika can talk to in the limited time she has, she's asked a friend to handle the logistical piece of the call—taking the individual's name, address, amount, and how they'd like to contribute (check, cash, charge). Whoever is helping, whether it's a friend or a member of your campaign staff, they'll also keep track of how much Patrizia has pledged, whether the money comes in, if a follow-up is needed, and how much Patrizia can still give under campaign finance laws.

You *can* learn how to raise money. As with anything, practice makes perfect. Say your pitch out loud to your cats/dogs/fish/succulents (we see you, millennials). Do practice calls with friends. Show up for a training offered by EMILY's List (see the next page) or take an online webinar to perfect your fundraising ask. There are also fundraising experts who work with women candidates to teach and refine the art of asking for money. But here is what can't be taught, and what *you* need to bring to the table:

★ A willingness to ask for money

★ A willingness to ask for more money

If you can say yes (or, let's be honest, at least "getting there" or "working on it") to these things, you're well on your way to being the most successful fundraiser in the history of the world.

YOU DON'T HAVE TO DO THIS ALONE

Depending on where you are running (as in super-local small town, big city, state-wide, etc.) you may have advisors, consultants, and staff on your campaign who are dedicated to helping you raise money. Look back at your Campaign Supporter List. Is there anyone on any of your lists who is a financial wizard? Anyone who has fundraised successfully? These people could become your fundraising chairs. Your finance director will help make lists of call sheets for you with names of donors who are likely to want to give to your campaign. She will also help you go through your Inner Circle and Community Circle to figure out how much to ask from each person. And, even better, she'll help keep track of all the money you're raising so that instead of being your campaign's accountant, you can simply focus on raising money and running for office.

The most important piece to remember is that there are people who will be working with you, alongside you, and for you who can help you raise the money you need to win. If you have a larger campaign, your team will do research about donors to help build lists of people you can call. They will advise you on how much to ask for. They will connect you to organizations and groups that help raise money for and make donations to candidates just like you!

One such group is EMILY's List.

THE STORY OF EMILY'S LIST

EMILY's List was founded in 1985 by Ellen R. Malcolm. She gathered a group of women who were committed to electing pro-choice Democratic women. Its name comes from the reality that women don't have access to the same financial networks as men do. EMILY is an acronym for **E**arly **M**oney **I**s **L**ike **Y**east . . . it makes the dough rise. Because women don't have the same access to networks of cash and power, they often can't raise the requisite funds early enough to be seen as viable and winning candidates, so the founders of EMILY's List created their own alternative network of women donors to support women candidates early in the process.

They wrote letters to all their friends in their Rolodexes (there's that word again!) and asked them to send donations for women candidates. The checks came pouring in. And a new, outside-the-boys'-club network for women candidates was born. EMILY's List has become the largest resource for women in politics. They've raised over $600 million for women candidates. They've helped elect 150 women to the US House, 26 to the Senate, 16 governors, and almost 1,100 to state and local offices.

But it's not the only organization dedicated to electing women. Others include Higher Heights for America (which works to elect African American women to office), LatinasRepresent, VIEW PAC (Value in Electing Women PAC, which works to elect Republican women), She Should Run, and VoteRunLead. Organizations focused only on state and local women candidates exist too. In Texas, there's Annie's List, and in Iowa, there's DAWN's List. Women in New York can rely on Eleanor's Legacy to help them run and win in their state.

All of these organizations offer a variety of invaluable resources like fundraising coaching, campaign trainings, online tools, and expert advice to help you run. Across the country, women are coming together to create space for themselves in politics. We'll talk more about organizations that can help you in Chapter Fourteen: THE HOLY BIBLE.

KEEP READING. STAY WORKING.

We need you.

I'm Running for Office.

THE CHECKLIST

1. I know why it's IMPERATIVE that more women run for office. ☐

2. I was nominated by _____.

3. Oh, hell yes, I'm qualified to run for office. ☐

4. I'm running for office to _____.

5. The office I'm running for is _____.

6. The filing deadlines for this office are _____.

7. The other requirements for this office are _____.

8. I have met those requirements. ☐

9. I've told these lucky people I'm going to run for office, because making this promise to myself and others matters: _____.

10. I've completed my week of self-promotion. ☐

11. I've built my Campaign Supporter List in a good ol'-fashioned spreadsheet. ☐

12. **My fundraising goal is $_____.**

JUNE

Use this space for notes on what you'll say in your fundraising calls.

KATE

She Believed She Could, SO SHE DID

Catherine Cortez Masto

Until 2016, the United States had never elected a Latina to the Senate. But that all changed when Democratic Nevada Attorney General Catherine Cortez Masto put her name on the ballot. The granddaughter of a Mexican immigrant, Catherine was born and raised in Las Vegas. Before she served as the state's attorney general, she was chief of staff for former Nevada Governor Bob Miller. She also worked as an assistant county manager in Clark County.

As attorney general, Catherine became known for her advocacy on behalf of seniors and women. She protected older Nevadans from identity theft, exploitation, and abuse. As the state's prosecutor, she broke up sex trafficking rings and worked to give first responders the necessary tools to identify trafficking. She also helped pass a law to make sex trafficking a state crime.

Catherine's longstanding commitment to women and girls has been front and center of her work in the Senate. She has sponsored bipartisan legislation to take on the human trafficking of Native Americans and Alaska Natives.

She's proposed legislation to promise coverage of preventative health care services, including breast cancer screenings and birth control. And she has cosponsored the Code Like a Girl Act to encourage girls to enter STEM fields like computer science.

While she was campaigning for the Senate, Catherine was inspired by the women she met, and she wanted to inspire them in return. She said, "The most important things are the incredible Latinas that I've met along the way, and young girls who are so excited when they meet me and know that I'm the first Latina. For me, that tells me they are looking at me saying, 'Oh my gosh, if she can do it, I can do it too.' And that's what I want them to think."

"I am here today to tell my faceless bullies that I cannot be shamed into quitting, because I am not ashamed."

———————

—SONOMA CITY COUNCILWOMAN
RACHEL HUNDLEY (D-CA)

Chapter Ten

WHAT ABOUT THOSE PESKY NUDES I TOOK?

AND OTHER QUESTIONS ABOUT LIFE ON THE INTERNET

What Did YOU Post?

★

What Have Others Put on the Internet About You?

★

What to Do About the Stuff You Can't Control

★

How Your Campaign Can Use the Internet for Good

★

Expanding Your Cyber Circle

emember the video of you and that uncomfortably middle-aged stripper from your cousin's bachelorette party? You were high on margaritas and sun damage and he threw your hands on the ground and then lifted you into something of a wheelbarrow, at which point he stuffed his face into your crotch while you screamed with laughter, shock, and delight? That wasn't posted online anywhere, right?

Right?

Most of us live our lives online. Facebook, Twitter, Instagram, Snapchat, YouTube, and, by the time you are reading this book, probably a slew of new platforms (MeetSnap, TitsSend, and Peepsbook—we just made those up, but consider them copyrighted!). We post pictures, videos, 280-character tweets. We stay connected with friends and family and people we don't much care for anymore.

As a candidate and public official, you will use the Internet too. You will communicate with voters, raise money, share stories, and rally the troops online.

We want to help you do that effectively. We also want to make sure your past posts don't have a chance to derail your campaign. We want to get you started on an inventory of your online presence, highlight the don'ts of social media, set your privacy settings, and help you figure out how to post with real purpose.

THE INVENTORY: WHAT HAVE YOU PUT OUT ON THE INTERNET?

Check off all the social media platforms where you have personal accounts.

❑ Facebook

❑ Twitter

❑ Snapchat

❑ Instagram

❑ LinkedIn

❑ YouTube

❑ Tumblr

❑ Google +

❑ Pinterest

❑ Myspace

❑ Friendster

❑ Dating apps (Tinder, Bumble, Thurst, HER, Match, OkCupid, eharmony, Grindr, PlentyOfFish, Coffee Meets Bagel, FarmersOnly, Zoosk, Christian Mingle . . .)

KATE

Yes, you've put public information about yourself on these dating sites.

Take an afternoon and review what you've posted on all of your accounts. And we mean really comb through. Consider each and every picture and post on every site to make sure the public record you've created for yourself is exactly what you want it to be now. For some of us, this may take more than an afternoon. You can do it! If you go to the accounts section of Twitter, you can request an archive of all your tweets. For Facebook, Instagram, YouTube, and the rest, you can either manually go through all your posts/pictures or see if the platform can send you an archive. Trust us, this is worth it. You will be looking for a few things:

1. Are there any photos that are . . . how shall we put this? . . . not what you would want an employer to see?

> *I remember posting a picture of me holding a margarita the size of my head. I'm definitely taking that down.*

MONIKA

2. Are there any statements that, in retrospect, you wish you hadn't made?

The statements don't even have to be about your vagina. Think about what each post might be saying to a potential voter.

Gracie
@Gracie

Vagina smells funny.

2 hours ago near

Gracie
@Gracie

Omg how do I remove posts from the cellphone??!?!?

2 hours ago · Like

Gracie
@Gracie

I just wanted to google it!!!

Alexandra H
@AlexanderH Nov 13, 2013 at 11:34pm ·

Is not looking forward to another day of people moaning at me!! #dontwanttogotowork

12 comments · 10 likes

Is this the attitude you want to see from your elected representatives? We don't think so.

3. Have any of your posts offended others? If they have, take stock of them: How do you feel about them now? If someone asked you about them today, what would you say? Do you regret making them? It is better to know what you said and decide how you'll respond if asked about it.

4. Have you posted private information? Home address? Phone number? Social security information?

5. Are there posts you've written or retweeted that are simply *not accurate*?

JustJeanine
@JustJeanine

my sisters pregnant I cant wait to find out if im gonna be an auntie or a uncle!!

2 hours ago

BaeB
@BaeB

finally got my debit card! Love the blue!!

5 hours ago • 238 Likes

BaeB
@BaeB

the back code of my card is 388 why is everyone asking? smh

Just now

You are the only one who is responsible for the veracity of your posts. So before you hit "send" or "publish," check the sources of the articles you want to retweet. Are you posting from a reputable news outlet or organization? Are you retweeting something that others have already debunked as false? We are praying the term "fake news" has been retired by the time this book is published, but if it hasn't, then make sure you aren't adding to the fire. Fact-check the news you choose to share. Google it. Do other media outlets confirm it? Still not sure if it's true? Then use snopes.com, factcheck.org, or politifact.com to see if any of them has anything to say on the matter.

Take time to consider each and every one of your posts. Assuming that everyone in the world can see what you have posted (spoiler alert: *they can*), are you comfortable with everything that's there?

TO DELETE OR NOT TO DELETE?

If you find posts you want to delete, then here's what to do: *delete them*. There is no shame in hitting that sweet delete button. Programs like the aptly named TweetDeleter and Twitter Archive Eraser can help.

If you are staring at a post and going back and forth on whether or not to delete it, then consider it a carton of milk. If you have sniffed it more than once, throw it out!

But even as you hit that delete button and start fresh, know that more than likely your online footprint will still exist, somewhere, somehow. People may have quoted your tweet, liked your post, saved it, or printed it for their scrapbooks. And remember, the Internet is written in ink, and all these past tweets are available on the dark web somewhere.

JUNE

Nothing scares me more than the dark web.

PRIVACY SETTINGS ARE YOUR FRIEND

Once you decide you're going to run for office, you can (and should) create "public" social media and email accounts. These are the accounts that you will use to tell people about yourself, where you can post campaign updates and messages about your platform, and where you'll share ways for people to donate. These accounts should be shared widely and openly. However, your private accounts should stay private. This is where privacy settings come in handy. Any social media platform worth your time will have a way for you to set up just who can see what. Go into each platform you use and take a look at your current privacy settings. For your private accounts, we recommend tightening your settings, because, after all, they are meant to be private.

Click on those friends and followers lists and make some hard choices. Do you still want to be connected to your ex–best friend from middle school who you are happy not to have spoken to for the past twenty years? Or what about the woman you met at the Fight for $15 rally? You didn't catch her name, but you totally accepted her Instagram request. You can let these people know to head on over to your public account to stay in touch and hear about your campaign. And then you can delete them from your private accounts!

Here is an example of what this might look like on Twitter or Facebook for Beth:

★ Private Account: BethLovesChardonnay36

★ Public Account: Beth for Iowa

On Instagram:

★ Private Account: WineLadyB!

★ Public Account: Beth for Iowa!

WHAT CAN PEOPLE FIND OUT ABOUT YOU?

Now that you've been able to take some control of what *you* put out there, it's time to see what else is out there about you online.

Start with doing a deep Google search of your name in quotes to see what's out there. If you've never googled yourself, we stand impressed and in awe of you.

KATE

Surprised that there's information about you online that's not on Facebook? Hold on to your butts.

Now that you've googled yourself, you are going to keep on googling yourself. If you don't have one yet, it's time to set up a Google Alert. The Google Alerts will essentially do a frequent Google search about you so you don't have to.

It's simple. Go to google.com/alerts, and then simply type in your name with quotation marks around it—for example, "June Diane Raphael" or "Kate Black." Google will scan the web for any items with your name in them (everything from random Medium posts or old Tumblr pages to Better Business Bureau reviews to RateMyProfessor.com ratings) and will send you an email to alert you. Here's one that June got.

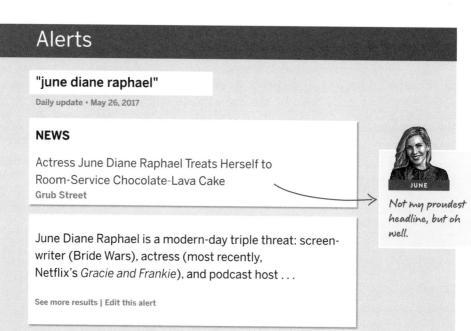

Alerts

"june diane raphael"

Daily update • May 26, 2017

NEWS

Actress June Diane Raphael Treats Herself to Room-Service Chocolate-Lava Cake
Grub Street

June Diane Raphael is a modern-day triple threat: screen-writer (Bride Wars), actress (most recently, Netflix's *Gracie and Frankie*), and podcast host . . .

See more results | Edit this alert

JUNE

Not my proudest headline, but oh well.

Google Alerts give you a chance to stay abreast of what's written about you. If you see something in a Google Alert that's concerning or that you would like taken down, and you know how to get in touch with the organization or person who posted it, then by all means go ahead and ask.

Kate got her start in politics doing **opposition and self-research** for candidates. This used to involve traveling to remote towns and counties to dig up public records and comb through libraries to find old newspaper stories. Researchers had to make friends at courthouses to find old lawsuits and arrest records; they also had to literally cut out newspaper stories and articles with scissors and glue them into binders (a literal version of "cut and paste"). Now almost everything is online. There are massive databases with millions of newspaper articles from small towns and big cities all over the world, waiting to be searched by name, date, or subject. Most municipalities, courts, and counties have put their public records on the Internet. Materials that took the researchers months to dig through can now take minutes for campaigns to compile.

VERY IMPORTANT WORD ALERT **Opposition and self-research** is research done on yourself and your opponent to highlight vulnerabilities and weaknesses in your/their records. It includes social media posts, public statements, voting history, public records like property documents or political contributions, and many other pieces of data. You can start some of this research yourself (hello, Internet inventory), but most larger campaigns will hire either staff or consultants to conduct this research and utilize it throughout the campaign.

There are databases and online services that scrape and scour the Internet at the speed of light and can deliver reports that include not only your social media activity, but every address you've ever lived at, your past employers, that time you accidentally registered as a member of the Green Party, and also really important things like whether you've paid your property taxes.

Remember, if you can find it, then a possible opponent, voter, or reporter can find it too. Also remember, everyone has a past and is concerned about something in it. Here's what Heather, Shawnta, Hilda, and Beth are worried about and what they can do about it.

HEATHER

I was arrested at Standing Rock. I have the arrest documentation, and if asked, I'm comfortable talking about that.

Knowing the details of your legal issues is important, but it's equally essential to be able to talk about the situation. What led to your arrest? What were you protesting? What are you continuing to fight for? Does it make sense to proactively include your arrest record in your campaign? All of these are questions to consider.

SHAWNTA

For a few years I didn't pay property taxes on a beach condo. The bills were being sent to the wrong address and I didn't think to check. Someone will find that out, right?

Yes, property tax payments are public record. Not only will people be able to see that the property tax payments were missed, but they will also see what late fees or penalties were assessed and if those were paid as well. Our advice? If you have unpaid taxes, work to get them paid as soon as you can.

HILDA

I've been fired from a job before. That's not online anywhere, is it?

The fact that you were fired from a job, performance reviews, and other occupation-related information used to be private. But now, thanks to the trusty Internet, we have Yelp, Glassdoor, salary.com, LinkedIn, and so many other websites where employees and employers can rate, review, post, and share their work experiences. So maybe you had to fire someone and it went poorly—did that person share their side of the story online? Have you, as the employee, ever posted about your current or former workplace? Do you provide a service, and do customers write reviews of that service?

It's always best to know what's out there regarding your professional history so that you can correct any errors, ask for posts to be removed, or consider how you would respond if someone brought up your review from four years ago of the pizza delivery guy who showed up an hour late. (You were hungry. You had your period. Your language was stark.)

BETH

I had an abortion when I was twenty-three. Is there a way for reporters to find out about it?

Personal health records are private and confidential. The only way for someone to know about your medical history is if you or someone involved disclose it or if it was part of a legal matter. If your medical history was part of a lawsuit, for example, that court record could be made available to the public.

Lucky for us, Kate created a handy cheat sheet of what's available as part of the public record and how to access it.

KATE

Medical records are confidential, but can confidential information leak? Sadly, yes.

TYPE OF RECORD	WHERE TO FIND IT	WHAT TO DO
Your Voter Registration (you are registered, right?)	Your secretary of state's website. Most states have a voter lookup tool to check where you're registered. If your state's webpage doesn't have an easy way to locate your registration, check your county board of elections.	Not finding yourself there? Get registered, baby! Voting is the most important thing you can do as a citizen! Registered with the incorrect party? Call your board of elections and get that corrected. Does this remind you that you might still be registered in another state where you used to live? Check that state's registration page. You should not be registered to vote in more than one state.
Your Voter History (showing when you voted, but not who you voted for)	This information is usually not online but can be requested at the county board of elections.	Did you miss elections? It happens. If you can request it, get a copy of your voter history mailed to you so you have it for your records. Check which elections the record says you missed: Did you actually vote and it's an error? Was it a presidential election or a local one?
Your Political Giving History (which candidates did you contribute money to?)	If you've contributed to federal candidates, you can search your name in the Federal Election Commission's online database. Anyone who has given more than $200 to a congressional or presidential candidate is recorded and posted online. States localities also track campaign donations. Check your secretary of state's or the local board of elections website to see who you've given money to in the past.	Does the FEC show you gave $500 to former pizza shop owner-turned presidential candidate Herman Cain in 2011? Be thoughtful about how you'd respond if asked about your donation. Perhaps you felt strongly about Cain's 999 plan, or maybe you've rethought your allegiance to it. Either way, obtaining your contribution records is the first step before you can move forward.
Property Records (mortgages, deeds, land trusts, property taxes)	These are typically found online at the county recorder of deeds, the registrar, or the tax collector.	Make sure you're up to date on your property taxes—note the next due date, and bookmark the page so you can easily find it again. Are you taking any tax exemptions? Are those exemptions correct? Have you bought or sold property in another state? Find those records and make sure they are up to date.

TYPE OF RECORD	WHERE TO FIND IT	WHAT TO DO
Personal Income Taxes	Unless you accidentally put your income tax filing on Instagram, these are not online. (But if you've been issued a lien or judgment to pay, the court record filed by the IRS will be publicly available.)	Are you up to date on your taxes? If not, can you work out a payment plan? Do you know an accountant or lawyer who can help?
Criminal or Civil Court Records (arrests, lawsuits, liens and judgments, marriages and divorces, probate issues . . . there are myriad reasons to check your name in the courthouse database)	Most cases can be found online via courthouse websites, but for older records, you might have to go to the courthouse in person and request copies.	If you have outstanding legal issues, consider hiring a lawyer—perhaps someone in your Inner Circle who can help? Get her up to speed on any legal issues you find and see what she can do to help get your case cleared. Records that were sealed in the process of the case (unless otherwise indicated) should remain sealed and should not be available to the public.
Debt (student loan payments, credit card debt, mortgage payments, car loans, etc.)	Unless you were taken to court to pay your debts, this information is typically not available to the public.	Some elected offices require you to file personal financial disclosure reports. These reports usually require a statement about your debt (how much you owe and to whom).
Medical Records	More and more of our medical histories (relating to both our mental and physical health) are moving out of paper files and into the digital world. But breathe easy; this doesn't mean they are online.	Unless any of your medical history is pertinent to a court case and is included in court records, it is unlikely that your medical records are available to the public.
Military Service Records	Some records pertaining to a veteran's dates of service, awards given and received, personnel documents, or medical history are available to the public and can be requested online from the National Personnel Records Center of the National Archives. But almost all records are released only to the veterans themselves or their next of kin and are not available to the public.	If you're a veteran and running for office, get a backup copy of all your records. That way you have the proper documentation should the press or anyone else ask for it.

Did you not only review the cheat sheet but search to see whether you come up on any of the sites? Did you find things you didn't know were out there about yourself? Maybe you found a lot of unpaid parking tickets? Breathe. It's okay. Voters know that people experience financial or legal issues—they are just like you. They respect the truth, because they've been there. But they won't understand if you try to hide it or don't acknowledge it. Find out what's out there about yourself. Then practice talking about these issues so that when you're asked, you're prepared. Remember, your experiences are what make you the most qualified candidate.

The bottom line is this: We can control all of what we ourselves put out on the Internet and some of what others do. And we should do both to the full extent that we can. Know that you can ask that old pages be removed. You can delete ancient Myspace accounts. And don't be afraid to ask friends not to post pictures if you don't want them to. This doesn't mean people will oblige, but it doesn't hurt to ask.

WHAT TO DO ABOUT THE STUFF OUT THERE THAT YOU CAN'T CONTROL

Although it may be easy to delete an old post or to ask a friend to take down a photo, there are things online that you simply can't request to be taken down. For better or worse, everything from legal documents to your campaign's personal finance reports to articles misquoting your views lives on the Internet. Any woman running will have to figure out how to handle what's out there about her. Knowing what's out there is the first step in figuring out how to respond.

Every situation is different, but when it comes to crafting your response, some general rules apply.

First, have all the facts. Do your best to gather all the requisite documentation, information, and facts about your specific situation. When and where did the arrest occur? Who did you first tell about the incident at work? On what date and time did you delete the problematic Facebook post? Arming yourself with facts will not only ensure you are telling the truth, but it will make you feel even more confident in telling your story the way it should be told.

Second, don't lie. Fudging the facts or making the truth sound better than it is will only dig you into a deeper hole. Voters may completely understand—and even relate—to your circumstance. But they don't respond well to politicians trying to cover up or hide information from them.

Next, decide what you want to say. For certain situations, like recovering from an addiction or something involving another family member, explaining that the situation is private and that you won't be discussing it on the campaign trail is completely sufficient. But for other situations, even though they may also be incredibly personal, sharing your story could help illustrate a larger issue that you care deeply about.

Need proof? Let us introduce you to Katie Porter and Stacey Abrams, and just *try* not to feel connected to them.

★ **Congresswoman Katie Porter (D-CA):** In 2018, Katie Porter, a law professor and mother of three, was running in a primary campaign for California's Forty-Fifth Congressional District. Years before her decision to run for office, she and her children had survived domestic abuse. But during her run, a whisper campaign began about her divorce and the protective order she requested against her husband. Then someone on Twitter referred to her as "Katie 'Restraining Order' Porter." Between the whispers and then the social media smear, Katie felt it was important to talk openly about her story. "I thought long and hard about this," she said to a reporter. "I think it's import-

ant that people understand that when real people run, they run with their real lives, and those lives might often include painful times." Along with providing all the legal documentation and details about her experience, Katie also told the reporter, "To be made to feel like I've done anything wrong—I'm just outraged. I have a wonderful track record. I've worked really hard to fight for consumers. That's what I should be campaigning on. But I'm not going to let someone, anyone, say that because a woman's been a victim of domestic violence, because she stood up for her children's safety, she's disqualified. Who will run then?" Katie went on to win her campaign by 12,500 votes.

★ **Former Georgia State House Minority Leader and Gubernatorial Candidate Stacey Abrams (D-GA):** In almost every campaign for any seat, candidates have to file a financial disclosure report, and that report is almost always made public. When Georgia gubernatorial candidate Stacey Abrams's report came out, there were questions about her personal credit card debt, outstanding student loans, and money she owed the IRS. To tell her story in the way that she wanted it told, she penned an op-ed that was published in *Fortune*, perfectly titled, "My $200,000 Debt Should Not Disqualify Me for Governor of Georgia." In the op-ed, Stacey described her

personal financial history—how she grew up in a working-class family, how during college her student loans and credit card debt increased, and how she had to take on financial responsibility for her family. In short, she had been where most Americans have been before. She wrote, "I am in debt, but I am not alone. Debt is a millstone that weighs down more than three-quarters of Americans. It can determine whether we are able to run for office, to launch a business, to quit a job we hate. But it should not—and cannot—be a disqualification for ambition."

Your story is *your* story. Don't let anyone else tell your narrative, your history, your experience differently than how *you* want it told.

AND FINALLY, THOSE PESKY NUDES

But wait, you say! What if it's worse than a disgruntled employee or legal settlements? What if it's nude photos or a sex tape that you're worried about? If they are on your own phone or computer, you may want to consider saving them to a secure hard drive or deleting them. If they are potentially on someone else's phone or computer—say an ex-boyfriend or ex-girlfriend or one-night stand—then what? Should you just give up the dream of public service right now? If the potential of a photo of sexual content becoming public is too horrifying, is it best to just stay in the private sphere of life and squash your passion and leadership potential?

> As a woman who has made a sex tape that may or may not make its way onto the Internet one day, I SAY NO! Stay the course. But you better believe this was one of the first questions I asked Kate when we spoke. I told her that I was fairly positive that the video made between me and an ex-boyfriend was destroyed, but that I couldn't be 100 percent certain and remain somewhat haunted by the idea of it ever gracing the World Wide Web. Although I would, of course, be honored to appear in anyone's masturbation material, I asked, "What would your advice be if I was your potential candidate?"

> I told June, if you can get the video back from your ex, then do so. But realize that he may have made a copy. If the worst-case scenario is that the video is leaked onto the Internet—

> Well, I think the worst-case scenario would be that it was leaked onto the Internet and no one watched it.

> Wow. Okay, if the worst-case scenario is that the tape is leaked onto the Internet, causing potential humiliation (maybe further still because it didn't go viral), then I would prepare a response. In my mind the strongest response is "The video is private and I will not be apologizing for or commenting on it."

> PREACH, BITCH, PREACH!

The truth is that the Internet can be a house of horrors for women. We are disproportionately harassed online, whether it's by revenge porn or threats on social media or trolling across the Internet, making us unsafe in the public space. As our lives become more and more uploaded, this issue is going to come up time and time again for women who are running for office. We know because it already has.

Shortly after Alejandra Campoverdi assumed the job of White House deputy director of Hispanic media in 2009, photos of her modeling for *Maxim* that had been taken years earlier were released, resulting in her being labeled the "White House *Maxim* Model." In 2017, Campoverdi ran for Congress in California and had this to say:

> *From this generation forward, every woman will have grown up in the digital age where, unless she sat in a turtleneck at home for all her teens, she will have pictures readily available online that can be used to shame her. And if these women decide to sit this one out because of that, we will miss out on talented, transformational women leaders in every public-facing field, especially politics. This will be a loss for our country and our future.*

> *Now more than ever, we must recognize and accept the complexity of real women and celebrate them in their quest for leadership roles. Whole, multidimensional women. Please throw your name in the arena, whichever one you're in—because it only gets better every time one of us tries.*

Yes yes yes, Alejandra!

And to the women who are not hiding any sexy modeling pics or the former porn stars or current sex workers who are reading this and have no desire to squash these photos or the public sexual space they occupy, we tip our hats and say: run, girl, run. You are making the expression of women's sexuality safer for all of us.

HOW YOUR CAMPAIGN CAN USE THE INTERNET FOR GOOD

Now that we've been pretty clear that the Internet is a dangerous place that has the ability to humiliate and degrade you, let's talk about its good side! Yes, it can be scary and awful, but it can also be the best thing to happen to your campaign.

You can use it to engage tons of people who could potentially be your voters, supporters, and donors. We're talking about good old-fashioned social media. And here's the great news: you don't have to travel to meet these people, and you don't have to pay for ads on TV and radio to get your message to them. You simply need a Wi-Fi connection and a social media account. As a candidate, the fact that most of the people who follow you will be people you've never met, yet who still want to be connected to you, is super valuable. Without knowing you, these people are already on board. And you never know where a new donor/supporter/voter will show up. Yes, even @IHaveHeadLice76.

So, assuming you have created public accounts and set privacy settings on your private, personal accounts, please answer the following questions about your public accounts.

How many Twitter followers do you have? _____

How many people do you follow on Twitter? _____

How many Instagram followers do you have? _____

How many Facebook friends do you have? _____

HILDA

I have fourteen Twitter followers, and two of those are my husband and my sister. This is bad, right?

These numbers are not just numbers. They are the people who are reading/watching/listening to what you are putting out into the world. You have direct access to them. They don't have a choice to return your calls or not. Unless, of course, they sneakily decide to mute you as opposed to blocking or unfollowing you. Rude.

Now you know how many followers you have. So how do you get more?

HOW TO GROW YOUR CYBER CIRCLE

Unless you're Selena Gomez or Barack Obama or Kim Kardashian, your online presence could be bigger and better. This is important, because when you run for office, you'll be communicating online—a lot. Here's how to do it.

1. Be authentic. Just as they do when you're talking face-to-face, people respond to authenticity online. It can be easy to edit two hundred characters to project a more perfect image of yourself. But we bet you'll find that it's the unedited, real ideas that move people to hit "like," retweet you, or go to your website to learn more about you.

2. Look at your profile pic. If your photo is of anything other than you—change it. A picture of the ocean tells a potential follower nothing about you, except that you like oceans. If that is your future campaign platform, that's awesome, but we still need to see *you*. Choose your favorite picture of yourself and get your face up there!

3. Make your bio work for you. Your bio does not have to be your entire résumé, but it does have to provide some information about who you are and what you find interesting. People are more likely to follow you if they like the same things you like. If you're already running, then the first thing should be what office you're running for and a link to your campaign website. If a campaign is in your future, don't hide it—put it in your bio! #FutureCandidate

4. Be active. Participate in conversations, retweet others, and tweet regularly. Over time this will help build a following. We're all busy—so thank god for apps. You can download apps like TweetDeck that allow you to schedule tweets to go out when you're away from your phone (which happens when, exactly?).

5. Identify who to engage. Are you following people who have a stake in your election? Who are influential in your community? Consider following groups who might support your campaign, as well as producers, journalists, local news reporters, community leaders, and other people you'd like to support you.

6. Engage. People will respond to your posts, so when you feel it's appropriate (see our thoughts below on engaging with trolls), engage with them! If someone asks a question about a policy position you hold, tell them what you believe. When a follower asks how they can help your campaign, tell them what time the phone banking starts and get them to bring a few friends!

7. Do not overuse the #hashtag. When someone is searching for a topic, using a proper hashtag will ensure they find you and will signal that you engage in this conversation on the regular. An insightful tweet about the future of women's rights could be found by others by using the hashtag #feminism. But adding twenty hashtags can confuse potential followers. Don't be that person.

YES, YOU NEED A WEBSITE

Even if you're running for the most local of local offices or president of the United States, you need a place on the Internet where people can go to find out more about you—from you! This is the place where you get to post your story, your experience, and your message about why you're the best candidate. And sidenote: it's also the place where people can give you money, sign up to receive campaign updates, and get in touch to volunteer for your campaign. Don't have the resources to buy an I'mRunningForOffice.com? Some social media platforms have candidate pages you can use to house a lot of this information. Start there!

8. Don't buy followers. Do not waste money on false friends. Work to get real ones—they will last longer. What's more, journalists are investigating and reporting on this practice. This is not something you want associated with your campaign.

9. Synergize. Post your Twitter account on your other platforms: LinkedIn, Instagram, Facebook, Snapchat! Wherever you are, let your audience know what other platforms you're also on.

10. Track it. Use the chart below to keep track of your followers and how you are engaging them (or not). Did you get a lot of followers when you discussed a plan to raise local taxes and used a Harry Potter GIF to make your point? Most social media sites have analytics platforms to help you see what posts connected with your followers, what messages worked, and where you grew the most. Use these tools to learn from that success and apply what you learn it in the future.

DATE	NUMBER OF TWITTER FOLLOWERS	NUMBER OF FACEBOOK FRIENDS	NUMBER OF INSTAGRAM FOLLOWERS	LESSONS LEARNED: WHAT WORKED? WHAT DIDN'T WORK?
Today:				
One month from now:				
Two months from now:				
Three months from now:				
Four months from now:				

JUNE

Yes, we are focused on the biggest online platforms (i.e., Twitter, Facebook, and Instagram). And yes, these platforms have problematic histories (i.e., data leaks, fake news, unregulated hate speech). But we are assuming that by publication date there will not have been a mass boycott and that most of y'all will still be on them.

By keeping track of when and how you grow your following, you'll know how to engage them later when they become potential supporters.

TROLLS AND WHY IT'S IMPORTANT NOT TO FEED THEM

Women face an unholy amount of harassment, misogyny, threats, and bullshit online. Some people might suggest avoiding social media completely. But if you're running for office (or running a business, or just living life), not having a social media presence is simply not an option. But what to do when the trolls come a-trollin'? Here are a couple of things to consider:

THING ONE: You've got a campaign/life to run and don't need to roll in the mud with the damn trolls. Reading that much negativity is not good for anyone. It's hard to ignore, but you can't let it impact your mission. So, as June would say, Don't Take It On.

THING TWO: If someone does harass or threaten you, you can Take It On by reporting them to the social media platform and the authorities.

Now that you've done your online inventory and learned the term "revenge porn," you are hopefully more prepared to respond to the puddle of shit the Internet can be and more prepared to use it for good for your campaign.

KEEP READING. STAY GOOGLE ALERTING. DON'T FEED THE TROLLS.

We need you.

I'm Running for Office.

THE CHECKLIST

1. I know why it's IMPERATIVE that more women run for office. ❑

2. I was nominated by _____.

3. Oh, hell yes, I'm qualified to run for office. ❑

4. I'm running for office to _____.

5. The office I'm running for is _____.

6. The filing deadlines for this office are _____.

7. The other requirements for this office are _____.

8. I have met those requirements. ❑

9. I've told these lucky people I'm going to run for office, because making this promise to myself and others matters: _____.

10. I've completed my week of self-promotion. ❑

11. I've built my Campaign Supporter List in a good ol'-fashioned spreadsheet. ❑

12. My fundraising goal is _____.

13. **I've done a full inventory of my online presence and set my damn privacy settings.** ❑

14. **When asked about any items found online about me (photos, arrests, etc.), I'm going to respond by saying:** _____.

> *You changed your privacy settings. Did you change your passwords, too? Do **not** write them here.*

JUNE

KATE

She Believed She Could, SO SHE DID

Lisa Murkowski

M-u-r-k-o-w-s-k-i. That's how you spell Murkowski. In 2010, Alaska voters learned how to spell Senator Lisa Murkowski's last name, because they had to write it in on the ballot.

Lisa had been serving in the US Senate since 2002, but in 2010, she lost the Republican primary election by just 2,006 votes. Lisa had a choice to make: Should she step aside, or should she stay in the game and mount a write-in campaign instead?

Lisa had received messages, notes, and calls from Alaskans urging her to keep up the fight and to mount a challenge. But the political pundits and consultants all said it couldn't be done. After all, a sitting senator hadn't mounted a successful write-in campaign since 1954. Moreover, they said it definitely couldn't be done in Alaska, where it would be hard to reach voters across a vast state and expensive to pull off.

Facing the toughest challenge of her political career, Lisa made her decision. She called her sister, who remembers the phone ringing. "I picked up the phone and said hello, and she said, 'Put on your big-girl pants—we're going to do this.'"

Over forty-five days, Lisa and her team educated voters on how to fill in write-in ballots and how to spell her name. Her first ad of the write-in campaign was called "Fill it in! Write it in! A Murkowski Public Service Announcement."

The PSA paid off. When the votes were counted, Lisa had won her long-shot victory and kept her seat in the Senate. We're thankful she did. Lisa has fought to protect a woman's right to choose, worked to keep the government up and running when others threw up their hands, and addressed the impact of climate change.

"[Congressmen] put the suit on . . . and get in front of a microphone and debate an issue. When we do it, it's, 'She's got nice shoes on.'"

—CONGRESSWOMAN RENEE ELLMERS (R-NC)

WHAT DO I WEAR?

The Inherent Sexism
in This Conversation

★

Choosing a Uniform

★

Finding What's Right for You

Kate, I'm nervous about this chapter.

 Talk to me!

 I think telling women how to dress is a slippery business. A woman's body is such a fraught area. We're graded and degraded. (By President Trump on a scale of 1 to 10. Literally.) Our bodies are politicized and are sites of sexual violence. And the clothes that we put on our bodies are judged constantly . . . I don't want to add to that, and I do not want to be in the business of telling women what to wear.

 But what if our reader wants help figuring that out?

 That ellipsis has come and gone about a million times over the last few minutes. What's happening to you over there?

 Sorry, I'm feeling a lot of feelings. I just don't want this section to seem prescriptive. I'm an actress, for Christ's sake—I'm always in a bit of a panic over how I look, my weight, my clothes, my hair, everything. And to be honest, Kate, I get really depressed about how much time I spend thinking about all this. I mean, what amount of my brain space would be freed up if I wasn't using it on my appearance?

 Okay, take a breath. But you also enjoy getting dressed up and generally love clothing and fashion . . . correct?

Oh, yes yes yes! I've fallen in love with many an instrument of my oppression ☺. Let me ask you— if I was running for office and came to you, Ms. Political Consultant, and asked you to dress me, what would you put on me?

Well, TBH, I would take you to Macy's or Bloomingdale's and we'd buy you a plain, dark suit, maybe a colorful jacket, a few blouses to go underneath, basic foundation garments (i.e., well-fitting bras), and some comfortable, sensible heels (god, I feel boring just saying that).

Something like this?

Ummm, no. I'm thinking something like this.

Oh, Kate, I can't wear that.

June Diane, I can see Jen An's boobs in the photo you sent.

And?

If she's running for office, that's really distracting. Wouldn't we want voters focused on other things besides boobs?

Distracting for whom? Why do we have to apologize for our breasts? If I want to give the people some cleavage, what is wrong with that? This whole subject is a giant pile of quicksand. I don't want to tell women that they have to tamp down their sexuality or, conversely, lose their modesty to have their voices heard. Our voices should be heard no matter what we are wearing or not wearing. I think we are in dangerous "she was asking for it" territory.

I hear you. I live in DC, and there is a uniform of sorts. Which is not necessarily a bad thing. For many women, a uniform can be really helpful—it means they can think less about what they're wearing and more about what they're doing. But for others, that uniform makes them feel less like themselves and more like an imposter. WHICH IS NOT THE GOAL. I think we can help the reader find a uniform that works for her.

I'm still scared, but yes, this sounds good. Also, how about this suit?

Can you imagine a world in which two men had that conversation? Probably not. Because for men this isn't an issue—they show up showered and in a suit, and voilà! they look like leaders. For us ladies, it's a different story. In the words of the great Nancy Meyers (filmmaker and creator of sick kitchen pornography) . . . it's complicated!

We acknowledge that this chapter is a sexist Bermuda Triangle, and by including it in the book we are intentionally flying right into it. Nonetheless, here we are. We're here because our goal is to give women all the tools necessary to make their run as easy as possible. Will that mean sharing research on what voters think of women candidates' clothing, hair, and makeup so that you, Dear Reader, can make informed decisions about your clothing, hair, and makeup? Yes, it will. Will we also encourage you to completely disregard this research if you please?

You better believe it. Will sharing the research also mean we are contributing to upholding the patriarchy, for now at least? Fuck. Yes, it will. We can play by the oppressive system's rules and dismantle it from the inside *or* we can throw the rules out altogether and dismantle the system. For now, we will do the former, but we reserve the right at any time to do the latter.

CAN WE REFER TO SOME RESEARCH, PLEASE?

Women candidates are judged by their appearance and held to a different standard than male candidates. Them's the facts, Jack. In 2016, the Barbara Lee Family Foundation, which has been working to understand the external obstacles women candidates face, found that "voters rated images of the more attractive officeholders more likeable, and found younger officeholders more attractive." Moreover, they found that "voters paid particular attention to women's appearance and race. This is especially true of women voters."

In 2013, a study, conducted by Name It, Change It, was done to test what happens in a campaign when a woman candidate's appearance is mentioned. Voters were asked to read about two candidates—one man and one woman. Then, some groups also read messages about the female candidate's appearance. Some of those messages were neutral in tone, some were positive, and some were negative. Here's the good news: before mentions of her appearance, the female candidate received 50 percent of the vote. But after voters read the positive descriptions of her appearance, the woman candidate's votes dropped to 43 percent. And after voters read the negative description, her vote total dropped again to 42 percent. So, any mention of her appearance hurts a woman candidate—with negative mentions doing slightly more damage than positive ones. *Great.* Again, let's stop talking about how our women candidates look.

JUNE

GOOD TO FUCKING KNOW!
When you find yourself judging another woman's appearance, stop and ask yourself why you're judging her. Instead of focusing on what women look like, listen to what they are saying.

Pramila Jayapal,
Washington Congresswoman

For Congress, I needed a whole new wardrobe and had to wear suits every day. As a woman of color, I also felt like I had to work twice as hard to get the credibility I deserved, so looking the part became that much more important.

MONIKA

> *How much is this going to cost me? I can't afford to buy a whole new wardrobe.*

SPENDING MONEY ON CLOTHES FOR YOUR CAMPAIGN

If you're running for federal office, you cannot spend campaign funds on clothing, hair, and makeup expenses. Running in local or state races? Be sure to check your state campaign finance laws before shopping. And know that if you do use campaign funds, the press, your opponent, and voters will be aware of those expenses, because they are publicly reported.

It's also important to be mindful of where your clothes are made. Ask yourself, was this made in the United States? Was this made under legal and ethical labor standards? These questions apply both to that amazing shift dress and to the T-shirts and other swag your campaign sells (which you will 100 percent be wearing, by the way).

Is it fair that women have to spend money, time, and energy on clothes and beauty to be seen as viable candidates—or more importantly, to not lose votes right off the bat because of their appearance? Absolutely not. Again, men can have a few suits and khaki pants and basically show up and lead. It costs a lot of time and money to present as a woman in our society, and those costs are a real barrier for women looking to lead.

Yes, women are judged more critically than men. And women of color are (again) further judged on the way they dress and look.

Let us be clear: we do not want to be in the business of telling women what to wear. We're not interested in adding to the pressure of having to "look a certain way." But we do want to be in the business of electing more women to office.

So in this chapter you are going to choose your own adventure. You are going to decide how *you* want to address the topic of what to wear as a candidate.

Adventure One: I THINK I'VE GOT THIS COVERED: If you feel awesome about your clothes and wearing them as a candidate, then a high five to you. You can stop reading now—and for the sake of all that is good, SKIP the rest of THIS CHAPTER!

Why are you still reading? Go on, get out of here!

Adventure Two: JUST GIVE ME A UNIFORM AND LET ME GET ON WITH MY LIFE: If you are pissed that we are spending so much time on the frivolous discussion of clothing and just want to go and buy what we tell you to buy so you can never think about this again, great. This is just the adventure for you.

Adventure Three: I HATE UNIFORMS—ESPECIALLY ONES THAT INVOLVE A SENSIBLE SUIT! If the idea of molding yourself to fit society's expectations for a candidate makes you uncomfortable, that's fine—there's a different adventure for you. (More on it in a bit.)

For those who chose ***Adventure Two***, here are Kate's candidate uniform suggestions:

A MODERN TAKE ON A PROFESSIONAL SUIT: Think a skirt and jacket, a blazer over a dress, or pants with a more fitted jacket. I'd advise a darker color, like navy or dark gray or, if you're really feeling it, dark purple, as your base. Don't be afraid of color when it comes to what you're wearing with your suits, jackets, or blazers! Blues, purples, reds, greens—who doesn't love a jewel tone?—all work.

TAKE INTO ACCOUNT WHERE YOU ARE CAMPAIGNING: Setting matters. If you're running in rural Montana, a pair of boots and jeans might be more practical and authentic to you and the community you're hoping to represent than a suit and high heels.

BETH

Hmm, most of my closet is business attire from my days as a TV reporter, so I have a lot of suits and bright blazers. What I need are casual clothes for campaigning in Iowa. A business suit doesn't sound like the right thing to wear when I meet local farmers.

OPT FOR COMFORT: Have a few options to go under your jackets. These can be blouses, shirts, or dresses that you'd be comfortable in if you had to take off your jacket. DO NOT wear something and think to yourself, "This works, as long as I don't take off my blazer all day." Whatever you're wearing underneath has to fit well, look appropriate for the events of the day, and be comfortable. Sleeves or no sleeves? Up to you.

CONSIDER MULTIPLES: Having a couple of blazers or jackets at the ready that are different colors but all work with your other clothes will make your suits last longer, because you'll be able to mix and match your blazers with pants or other skirts. Before you buy a jacket or blazer, make sure it will coordinate with your existing blouses and dresses that you would wear underneath.

★ Consider having a small section of your closet that is dedicated to your campaign so that when you're running, you can spend less time rummaging through your closet for that one item.

★ Will you have time to change during the day between campaign stops and visits? It's never a bad idea to have a second outfit at the ready in your car and in your office.

★ Pack a go-bag for your car that has emergency fashion supplies just in case of spills, clothing tears, or blisters from wearing those damn new shoes that looked so good at the store but are hell on the campaign trail. In your go-bag:

- Band-Aids for said blisters
- Tide to Go pen for small stains and spills
- Small sewing kit, safety pins, and/ or fashion tape for broken buttons, tears, or loose hems
- Deodorant for hot days
- Small containers of hairspray and dry shampoo
- Small makeup kit with just the essentials (not your full beauty bar from home)—just enough to touch up foundation, lips, cheeks, and eyes.

HEMLINE SUGGESTIONS: When you put on a skirt or dress that feels too short, it probably is too short. Do the stand up/sit down test. Is your skirt or dress fine when standing, but when you sit, all of a sudden more of your upper thigh is showing than you're comfortable with? That's a good enough reason to opt for something with a slightly longer hemline.

SHOES: First and foremost, it's a good idea to wear them. Second, if you're a woman who is 100 percent comfortable wearing heels all day, every day, get some that are not too high (under three inches) and that are extra comfy (or use inserts to add some cushion). If heels are not for you—nothing but respect—then have a few pairs of professional flats or very low heels (an inch or so) on hand.

SHAWNTA

Because I'm always talking to or working with vets, I usually wear my boots or my running shoes. Maybe it's time to get some new footwear.

INVEST IN FOUNDATIONS: This is a grown-up word for underwear/shape wear/bras. Take stock of what you currently have—if anything could fit better or no longer fits, consider buying new bras and underwear that help make your clothes look the best they can. June swears by the bra saleswomen at Nordstrom.

Voters want you to be a relatable everywoman, but they also want you to look the part. It's a delicate balance. As a black woman, I have had to negotiate how often and how drastically I change my hairstyle. . . . Part of the reason I choose to wear my hair in twists or braids is because I know there are women, particularly black women, who see their personal style as being contrary to what we've come to believe politicians or other professional women are supposed to look like. I think all women, regardless of their hair or personal style, should be able to look in the mirror and say "I look like a politician."

Ayanna Pressley,
Massachusetts
Congresswoman

The idea of getting fitted for a bra creeps Kate out. To each her own. Whether you buy them in person or go online, getting foundation garments that fit and make you feel your best is key. Do not spend all this time and effort putting together a legit candidate outfit and then put on the seven-year-old bra that you swear is lucky and fits perfectly. It isn't and does not.

Below are some outfits Kate thinks work as potential candidate uniforms. If you already have these in your closet, great. If not, it's time to make a trip to your nearest department store.

Clothes are self-expression for me, so I try to dress in what makes me comfortable— both fit-wise and personality-wise. But during a campaign, days are especially long and require you to be in all sorts of settings, so I would advise keeping outfits basic and comfortable.

Liz Brown, Columbus City Councilwoman

Adventure Three: THE UNIFORMS YOU DESCRIBED MAKE ME UNCOMFORTABLE TO MY CORE, but I still don't know what to wear. If the idea of putting any of the previous lewks (or "looks," for the older and wiser set) onto your body feels incredibly "not you," that's totally fine. Let's go a different route.

Head to your closet and take a look at what's already there. Let's make your own style work for you, the candidate. Select a few options for an outfit that you would wear to go get your dream job. Let's ask Heather and Hilda what they'd pull out.

My nurse scrubs and Dansko black clogs.

HEATHER

Okay, Heather, good point. Select some clothes you would wear to a nice dinner with friends.

Hilda, what's in your closet?

A sundress that's got buttons and a collar, plus a woven belt with some low-heeled sandals.

HILDA

Got to say, Hilda—that outfit sounds perfect for campaigning.

As a candidate you are going to be interviewing for a job every day. You'll be meeting with voters in boardrooms, on the street, in coffee shops, in union halls, at diners, and at cocktail parties. You'll have to be presentation-ready at all times. Choose the clothes in your closet that you think show you in your best light.

CHANGING WHAT A POLITICIAN LOOKS LIKE

Women candidates and leaders have been judged for their appearance since the beginning of time. But the good news is that the times, they are a-changin'. As more and more women run for office, they are changing voters' minds about what a politician can look like. Women who are running up and down the ballot are choosing their own adventures when it comes to their appearances and not holding themselves to unfair expectations or limitations on how they express themselves and their identities.

We don't need to shy away from what we want to wear, because as more women run for office—especially more young women and women of color—they create more options for what leadership can look like. Some leaders wear more traditional suits, and others step out of the box. Some wear board shorts; others, ruffled jackets or leather. Whether you wear a head scarf, zebra-print hat, or rock a popped collar, you can change what being a woman candidate looks like *just by wearing what you want to wear.*

Now let's stop talking about clothes. Let's just wear the clothes and get the fuck on with it.

KEEP READING. STAY WORKING.
We need you.

I'm Running for Office.

THE CHECKLIST

1. I know why it's IMPERATIVE that more women run for office. ❑

2. I was nominated by _____.

3. Oh, hell yes, I'm qualified to run for office. ❑

4. I'm running for office to _____.

5. The office I'm running for is _____.

6. The filing deadlines for this office are _____.

7. The other requirements for this office are _____.

8. I have met those requirements. ❑

9. I've told these lucky people I'm going to run for office, because making this promise to myself and others matters: _____.

10. I've completed my week of self-promotion. ❑

11. I've built my Campaign Supporter List in a good ol'-fashioned spreadsheet. ❑

12. My fundraising goal is _____.

13. I've done a full inventory of my online presence and set my damn privacy settings. ❑

14. When asked about any items found online about me (photos, arrests, etc.), I'm going to respond by saying: _____.

15. **I absolutely know what I'm going to wear as a candidate. ❑**

JUNE

KATE

Use this space to jot down some of your political style icons. Olivia Pope? Selina Meyer?

She Believed She Could, SO SHE DID

Elise Stefanik

In 2014, Elise Stefanik was elected to the House of Representatives for the Twenty-First District of New York. At thirty years old, she was the youngest woman ever to have been elected to Congress up to that point. If you see her in Washington today, you'll find her walking the halls of the Capitol. But when she leaves the office, more than likely she'll be driving her Ford F-150 pickup truck.

Elise has always brought her own mix of upstate New York roots to DC After graduating from college, she worked for President George W. Bush's Domestic Policy Council and led economic and domestic policy for Josh Bolten, the White House chief of staff. During the 2012 presidential campaigns, she was the director of debate preparation for vice presidential candidate Paul Ryan, and she helped write some of the Republican National Committee's platform.

The results of the 2012 election are what spurred Elise to consider running herself. She wanted to see different sorts of candidates running for office, especially in her home state of New York. She said, "I think . . . people were looking for new types of candidates who would think outside the box and who would work across the aisle on a bipartisan basis. I don't look like a typical candidate, but I think I have a lot to add."

In 2014, after moving home to work at her family's small business, she decided to run for Congress. No Republican had won her district in almost twenty-one years. Her campaign wasn't without challenges. Her opponent questioned her résumé and qualifications and threw a fair bit of shade on the young, single woman. But on election night, Elise overcame the sexist and baseless attacks. She won by 24 points. In her victory speech, she said, "I am honored and humbled to be the youngest woman ever elected to the United States Congress, and to add an additional crack to the glass ceiling for future generations of women here tonight."

"I think when people see young women running who have a lot of other things going on—I have a family; I have a job that I'm passionate about, a busy job—they think, 'There's no way she would put this into the equation of her life unless there was something that she wanted to die on the cross for.'"

———

—LETITIA CLARK, TUSTIN CITY COUNCILWOMAN (D-CA)

Chapter Twelve

BUT SERIOUSLY, HOW WILL THIS WORK IN MY REAL LIFE?

PART ONE

Do You Have the Time?

★

Can You Afford It?

O kay—you know what office you're running for and how much money you need to raise. You've figured out the basic elements of your platform and how to make social media work for you. But what about the biggest question of all?

How the hell will this work in my real life?

This is the question that paralyzes most of us. As we well know, women's real lives are women's full lives. We are working jobs and launching and sustaining careers. We are running households. We are taking care of children (small and not so small), and elderly parents and friends as well. We are volunteering and supporting causes we believe in. We are taking care of ourselves. And we are usually doing all of these things at once.

We are, as a whole, stretched.

And so how do we fit a campaign and then, god willing, a term in public office into our lives? In this chapter and the next, we're going to look at your time, your money, your career, the care you give, and the care you need to figure out how a campaign and elected office can fit into your life.

Running for office is such a commitment, and you need to be prepared for what that means to your financial life, your home life, and your social life. I had to put entire parts of my social life on hold because it was just more important for me to use that time to be elsewhere, attending events, talking to people, and being seen around the community.

DO I HAVE TIME FOR THIS?

Let's start with what most us feel we don't have enough of: time. Running for office takes time. Raising money, talking to voters, appearing at events, raising more money—all of this takes time.

How much time? Unfortunately, there's no equation that you can punch in to a calculator to find that answer. There are too many variables: where you're running, what you're running for, how much money you need to raise. That said, one way to figure out how much time your campaign will require is by asking someone who held the seat before you. If you have a connection to such a person, take them to coffee and ask how they did it, how many hours they put in, and any other lessons they learned. Some campaigns may take only some of your time, and others may require every one of your waking hours.

Most small, very local races will not require every minute of your day. If your race is bigger and on a larger scale—like a statewide race or a federal campaign— you're looking at spending almost all (if not all) your time on your campaign.

> My campaign for governor will take all of my attention, focus, and time. I've got to raise millions of dollars and build a statewide team of staff and volunteers, and spend time meeting with and engaging with voters! Hell, visiting each of Iowa's nearly one hundred counties alone will take hours upon hours of driving! I'm not sure I would have ever been able to take time off from my work to do this, but now that I'm retired, I can definitely make the time.
>
> **BETH**

If you need to raise a significant amount of money, you'll have to spend time making calls, attending fundraisers, and engaging your community. If the district you're running for is large and expansive, you'll have to spend time traveling from one end of it to the other.

KATE

Facing a lot of driving? Look at your Campaign Supporter List and see if there is anyone on it who can drive you while you make calls to supporters. Your retired neighbor? Your newly licensed nephew?

No matter what size your race is, you'll need to spend time reaching voters.

Do you have enough of it? The first step is to figure out what we are currently doing with the hours available to us. To do that, we'll log everything we do for two full weeks. We know that sounds like hell, but this particular exercise has proven to be the most revelatory when considering a run for office.

Here's a snapshot of how June did it.

JUNE

Where Does the Time Go?
JUNE'S TIME LOG

Wednesday

5:00–8:30 a.m. Older son Gus wakes SUPER EARLY bc of time difference from NY. (We got back to LA from NY last night.) Until Juliana, our nanny extraordinaire and the light of my life, arrives at 8:30, I (along with a truly wonderful husband) play with trains, get Gus ready for school, make waffles, and have breakfast with both kids.

8:30–8:50 a.m. Juliana (aka the cavalry) arrives. Get ready—dressed, makeup, hair in a bun.

8:50–9:05 a.m. I purchased several dresses for the Austin TV festival. I need to get the ones I didn't wear BACK IN THE MAIL today, otherwise I can no longer return them. Pack them up and print label.

9:05–11:00 a.m. Unpack myself and kids (we've been away for a week). Also unpack suitcase from a previous trip to Austin. Take a fifteen-minute break to watch Insta stories. Listen to a podcast. Put on *Real Housewives of New York* while I'm unpacking. I'm shocked they spend so little time on Lu's wedding. Please don't focus on why it took me two hours to unpack.

11:00–11:50 a.m. Talk to therapist on the phone while unpacking. Unpacking both emotions and physical items related to trip.

11:50–12:40 p.m. Can't read my own handwriting as I am transcribing this. WE WILL NEVER KNOW WHAT HAPPENED!

12:40–1:35 p.m. Pick up Gus from preschool. Because he is a nightmare from jet lag, I offer him a quick trip to Pinkberry (I want it too). We arrive there and I realize I don't have my wallet. We head home. I tell Gus I'm going to leave him with Juliana while I work in our guesthouse. I promise him he can come out back and give me a hug before his nap.

1:35–3:45 p.m. Emails. Work. Phone calls.

3:45–4:15 p.m. Wake Gus from nap. He is upset and only wants to be with me. I cave and agree that because I'm not "writing" but responding to emails and catching up on things, he can play in the guesthouse while I'm at my computer. This will prove to be a mistake.

4:15–6:00 p.m. Respond to emails. Work on my Pinterest board for Baby Sam's birthday party and order supplies/decor for it. Emails etc. Look at Insta stories and stare at shared photos from the vacation we just got back from.

6:00 p.m. Juliana leaves.

6:00–8:00 p.m. Bath, dinner, bedtime, etc. Kids are going to bed later because of jet lag!

8:00–8:15 p.m. Did I mention I came back from NY with a sinus infection? I get in the steam shower to try to help it.

8:15 – 8:45 p.m. Watch John Oliver.

8:45 p.m. Asleep.

Thursday

4:10–5:00 a.m. Gus is awake. What the fuck is happening? Time difference is killing us. I bring him into bed with me. I can't go back to sleep.

5:00–5:30 a.m. Find phone. Lie in bed and stare at phone like an undead zombie.

5:30–6:45 a.m. Sneak out of bed. Make coffee. Do a *New York Times* crossword. Read Twitter. Scour through "Randy Bryce for Congress" website. Read *New York Times*.

6:45–8:00 a.m. Gus and Sam both awake. Get them dressed, etc. Breakfast. They watch *Paw Patrol*.

8:15–9:30 a.m. Take a boxing class for parents at Gus's preschool. Husband stays with kids in preschool playground while I work out.

9:30–10:15 a.m. Juliana arrives. Get ready for day. Shower, etc.

10:15–10:30 a.m. Call with my lawyer re: book contract.

10:30–11:00 a.m. Drive downtown to Senator Kamala Harris's in-state office for a meeting with Indivisible LA.

11:00–11:30 a.m. Park VERY FAR AWAY and walk what feels like a million miles to office. Wearing the wrong shoes for this.

11:30–12:45 p.m. Meet with Senator Harris's aides to discuss health care bill.

12:45–2:00 p.m. Head back in direction of car. Can't remember where I parked. Takes a while to find car. Get a Starbucks in the hopes of calming my brain so I can remember where car is. Find car. I have a ticket on it. Drive to Paramount Studios.

2:00–2:45 p.m. Rerecord some dialogue for *Grace and Frankie*. Talk to writer about the season we have just wrapped.

2:45–3:00 p.m. Drive to coffee shop Alcove in Los Feliz to meet friend and fellow activist Jess Zaino.

3:00–4:30 p.m. Discuss potentially partnering with Jess on the Jane Club (the mother of all work spaces).

4:30–5:00 p.m. Realize I don't have any cash to pay the valet. Drive to bank. A theme of not having money on my person is clearly emerging.

5:00–6:30 p.m. Home. Juliana leaves. Sit with boys during dinner, bath. Husband will put them to bed.

6:30–9:00 p.m. Dinner with producer friend to catch up and discuss upcoming projects.

9:00 p.m. Home. ASLEEP.

And here's a sample of how Kate logged her time.

KATE

Where Does the Time Go?

KATE'S TIME LOG

	TUESDAY	WEDNESDAY	THURSDAY	FRIDAY	SATURDAY
7:00 a.m.	Coffee, litterbox, get dressed	Leave the house	Leave the house	Leave the house	Wake up, get dressed
7:30 a.m.	Leave the house	Arrive at office	Arrive at office	Arrive at office	Coffee, leave house
8:00 a.m.	Arrive at office	Work	Work	Work	Yoga
8:30 a.m.	Work	Work	Work	Work	Yoga
9:00 a.m.	Work	Work	Work	Work	Brunch with Allison
9:30 a.m.	Work	Work	Work	Work	Brunch with Allison
10:00 a.m.	Work	Work	Work	Work	Brunch with Allison
10:30 a.m.	Work	Work	Work	Work	Target and shopping
11:00 a.m.	Work	Work	Work	Work	Target and shopping
11:30 a.m.	Work	Work	Work	Work	Target and shopping
12:00 p.m.	Work	Work	Work	Work	Target and shopping
12:30 p.m.	Work	Work	Work	Work	Target and shopping
1:00 p.m.	Work	Work	Work	Work	Target and shopping
1:30 p.m.	Work	Work	Work	Work	Snack, discuss life plans with Sam
2:00 p.m.	Work	Work	Work	Work	Snack, discuss life plans with Sam
2:30 p.m.	Work	Work	Work		Snack, discuss life plans with Sam
3:00 p.m.	Work	Work	Work	Call with Jess	Laundry
3:30 p.m.	Work	Work	Work	Watch *Great British Baking Show*	Nap

	TUESDAY	WEDNESDAY	THURSDAY	FRIDAY	SATURDAY
4:00 p.m.	Work	Work	Work	Watch *Great British Baking Show*	Nap
4:30 p.m.	Work	Work	Work	Contractor meeting at house	Nap
5:00 p.m.	Work	Work	Work	Meet friends and Sam for drinks	Nap
5:30 p.m.	Work	Gym	Work	Meet friends and Sam for drinks	Shower
6:00 p.m.	Work	Gym	EL Happy Hour	Meet friends and Sam for drinks	Watch *Great British Baking Show*
6:30 p.m.	Meet Meghan for drinks	Grab drink with Geri	Home, wine and TV	Dinner	Watch *Great British Baking Show*
7:00 p.m.	Meet Meghan for drinks	Grab drink with Geri	Home, make dinner with Sam	TV time	Get changed for dinner
7:30 p.m.	Meet Meghan for drinks	Grab drink with Geri	Litterbox, laundry	TV time	Leave for date night
8:00 p.m.	Home, make dinner	Home, dinner	TV time	Reading	Date night
8:30 p.m.	Watch reruns of *West Wing*	More *West Wing* reruns	TV time	Reading	Date night
9:00 p.m.	Watch reruns of *West Wing*	More *West Wing* reruns	Reading	Bed	Date night
9:30 p.m.	Comment on chapters	Call with Sam	Bed		Date night
10:00 p.m.	Comment on chapters	Comment on chapters			Date night
10:30 p.m.	Bed	Comment on chapters			Date night
11:00 p.m.		Bed			Date night
11:30 p.m.					Date night

So it seems that, yes, we are two very different personality types. But as you can see, we each got a sample of two weeks of our lives.

We then broke down our activities into categories so we could see how we spent our hours each day over a two-week period. We totaled the number of minutes and averaged them out to see what a "typical"—if such a thing exists—day looks like. For us, a "typical" day looks something like this:

TIME LOG ANALYSIS		
	KATE	**JUNE**
Paid Work	8 hours, 30 minutes	4 hours
Self-Care	1 hour, 35 minutes	1 hour, 18 minutes
Family Care		6 hours, 36 minutes
Free Time	2 hours, 12 minutes	54 minutes
To and From	1 hour, 48 minutes	1 hour, 24 minutes
Housekeeping	42 minutes	8 minutes
Partner Care	1 hour, 36 minutes	24 minutes
Career Investment	4.2 minutes	1 hour, 18 minutes
Volunteer		36 minutes

A note about the categories: These are categories that we picked for ourselves. To us, "self-care" included going to the gym, therapy, and meditation. "Free time" included watching reruns of *West Wing*. "To and from" represented time spent driving or otherwise getting from point A to point B. As you're looking at your time, you can use our categories or create different ones that better fit your life. By staring at this daily analysis, we realized a few things about our lives: June does not have a lot of free time and Kate's home is a lot cleaner than June's.

Using this analysis, we could clearly see where and how we could create more time for a potential run for office.

JUNE

After looking at the chart and some deep introspection, I realized the biggest chunk of time per week for me is childcare—spending time with my small children. I am willing to cut about an hour out of that time each day, but no more than that. These years with them are precious to me, and if I can afford to be with them, I want to. I can't budge on the paid work time because I need to support myself and my family, and I know that I need the self-care time. I could lose the free time altogether and lose the volunteer time and career investment time, and obviously the housekeeping time has to go. (I know it's only 18 minutes a day, but still, it CAN GO!) So, in total, I'm freeing up almost 3 hours.

Kate, is that enough for me to run for, let's say, neighborhood council?

Probably! Neighborhood councils are like mini boards of advisors that assist the city council. Some are volunteer, and some you can run for. Given that the geographic region is small (i.e., it's your neighborhood) and that you likely know most of the voters, I think you could make this work. Plus, you could bring the kids with you while you knock on some doors!

KATE

JUNE

Okay, this is good to know. It was helpful to quantify my schedule and realize that a run for neighborhood council is possible (I have a lot to say about what's going on with the stop sign situation here). You?

Looking at my chart, I realized that I could reduce my free and career investment time (yes, all 4.2 minutes of it) and reduce my self-care time. But if I were to run for office, especially federal office, that still wouldn't create enough time to raise money and talk to voters. I would have to seriously consider leaving my job to campaign full-time. But knowing this helps me think about how a campaign could work in my long-term career plan.

KATE

Notice that Kate works a majority of her time in an office and June is a freelancer whose schedule is much less predictable. (June actually did three weeks of analysis to account for this, but with variable shooting schedules and some months being busier than others, her time was harder to quantify.)

So that's how we analyzed our time and figured out how much of it we need to run for office and what we would need to do to make a run possible. Want another example? Here's how **Heather** did it.

JUNE

If you have a schedule that is not at all consistent from day to day, you might want to inventory a few more weeks to get a more accurate average.

STEP ONE: She logged her time over the course of two weeks to figure out how she was spending it.

STEP TWO: She categorized her time log to see exactly how many hours she was spending and on what.

HEATHER

I'm at the hospital for three very long days a week, and the rest of the week I look after my mother-in-law.

STEP THREE: She considered how much time her run for Congress might require.

STEP FOUR: She figured out how much time she could free up to run for office and charted a plan of action.

STEP FIVE: She considered how her time would look if (or rather when!) elected.

She then came up with the following plan.

HEATHER'S PLAN			
CURRENT TIME	**TIME NEEDED FOR RUN**	**ACTION PLAN**	**FUTURE TIME**
As a registered nurse, Heather works twelve-hour shifts three times a week at the local hospital. She also spends four days a week caring for her mother-in-law. This is unpaid.	Heather needs to spend 100 percent of her time raising money, communicating with voters, and traveling all over North Dakota.	Talk to her union representative about negotiating a leave of absence that will enable her to return to her job after the campaign, if necessary. She will ask friends and family to care for her mother-in-law.	If elected to Congress, Heather's time will be devoted to traveling between North Dakota and Washington, DC, in order to best serve her community. She will not be working as a nurse or caring for her mother-in-law.

HEATHER

I recognize that running for Congress will be a full-time job. I'm thrilled at the support of my union in helping me negotiate a leave of absence from nursing—this is why unions matter, people! Handing over the care of my mother-in-law to other people—even people I trust—is harder for me. My mother-in-law is supportive and is even demanding that I do this. But it still has brought up some guilt.

Here's what **Shawnta** had to say after completing the Five Steps.

I love working with veterans every day but know that my usual nine-to-five job at my nonprofit will have to shift in order for me to run for city council. My support staff is going to be a huge part of my action plan as I cut down on a few hours at work. Also, I usually need a few hours to decompress at night after my daughter goes to bed at seven, but now I'm going to reroute that free time into campaign time.

SHAWNTA

Hilda works as a mom twenty-four hours a day. She also wants to run for Los Angeles County Board of Education. After completing the Five Steps, she realizes that she has to devote at least 75 percent of her time to running for office. But she also wants to safeguard her time with her kids. She comes up with this action plan.

I want my campaign to be an example of how to value mothers. My action plan is that I won't start campaign activities until 8:30 a.m. and won't schedule campaign work between 5 p.m. and 7 p.m. so I can be home for dinner and bedtime. I'm going to be honest with voters about the needs of working moms and why I'm choosing to campaign this way. I understand that if elected, voters will expect me to work full-time for my salary. But I also want to open up a conversation around working mothers, reasonable hours, and balance in the workplace.

HILDA

These women are making decisions about their time that only they can make. So now it's up to you to take a look at your life. In five definitely-not-simple steps, let's figure out how **you** can create the time for your run.

STEP ONE: Log your time. Use the worksheet on the next page or any other system that works for you.

STEP TWO: Study your worksheet and categorize how you spend your time. At the end of two weeks, total the number of minutes you've spent in each category and find your daily average.

TIME LOG ANALYSIS	
	DAILY AVERAGE
Paid Work	
Self-Care	
Family Care	
Free Time	
To and From	
Housekeeping	
Partner Care	
Career Investment	
Volunteer	

STEP THREE: Consider how much time your run for office might require. Although there is no magic number of hours you need to spend on your campaign, bear in mind that the size of your race, the money you need to raise, and the geography of the district will help determine that number. Remember, you can ask for help

TIME MANAGEMENT WORKSHEET							
TIME	Sunday	Monday	Tuesday	Wednesday	Thursday	Friday	Saturday
7:00							
8:00							
9:00							
10:00							
11:00							
12:00							
1:00							
2:00							
3:00							
4:00							
5:00							
6:00							
7:00							
8:00							
9:00							
TIME	Sunday	Monday	Tuesday	Wednesday	Thursday	Friday	Saturday
7:00							
8:00							
9:00							
10:00							
11:00							
12:00							
1:00							
2:00							
3:00							
4:00							
5:00							
6:00							
7:00							
8:00							
9:00							

from people who have run before, or you can do some researching online. How many hours a week—full-time (40 or more hours a week) or part-time (10 to 30 hours a week)—will you have to find in your schedule?

Hours per week needed for campaign: _____

_____

STEP FOUR: Look at your time log analysis. Where can you free up time? Could you enlist friends and family to help with family care? Housekeeping? Think about the paid work you do. Is it possible to reduce your hours or take a leave of absence? (For now, leave the financial hit you'd take out of the equation—we'll

BREAKING NEWS: WOMAN CAMPAIGNS WHILE BEING A MOM

When Kathy Tran decided to run for the Virginia House of Delegates in 2016, she made the choice to integrate her family fully into her campaign.

Kathy is a refugee from Vietnam who came to the United States when she was very young. Concerned about immigration, she decided to run for Virginia's House of Delegates. But she knew her family would have to be central to her campaign. Her fourth child, Elise (her first name was inspired by Ellis Island, and her middle name, Minh Khanh, is Vietnamese for "bright bell," was inspired by the Liberty Bell), was born one month before Kathy decided to run for office. When Kathy became a candidate, she tied her tennis shoes and picked up her baby carrier, and together, she and her infant daughter knocked on more than three thousand doors.

Kathy, with Elise in tow, met with voters and discussed issues like the environment and local schools. One report on her family-focused run for office stated, "As she talked to neighbors about traffic congestion and education, her daughter cooed and kicked her legs."

Kathy's family—her husband and three other children—canvassed together on weekends, because Kathy wanted her kids to know she was doing everything she could to make the lives of the next generation, their generation, a little bit better.

KATE

Kathy won her election in November 2017 by over 20 points. I'm not crying. You're crying.

look at that starting on page 175.) What else would you set aside, at least temporarily? Be honest with yourself.

For some women, if they don't make time for self-care (exercise, meditation, therapy), then NOTHING ELSE in their lives works. If that's the case for you, make that time sacred. Similarly, moms like June and Hilda may determine that time with their kids is nonnegotiable. Reserve time for the most important things in your life. However, you may need to find other aspects of your life that have to give.

How much time can you commit to freeing up? And what time do you need to preserve?

I'm going to cut ____ hours from _____ category to free up time for my run.

I need to protect ____ hours in _____ category to make my run possible.

Are there more hours and/or categories of time you want to protect or cut? Write them in here:

TIME I MUST PROTECT:

TIME I CAN LET GO:

STEP FIVE: If (or rather when!) elected to the office you are running for, how will your time change?

Ways my time will change: _____

This is a section you can continue to come back to and refine. As we discuss your money, your career, and the care you give/need, you may be able to free up more or less time. Because truthfully, we need more women in office yesterday, so we don't have the time to *not* figure this out.

CAN I AFFORD TO DO THIS?

And now it's time to discuss the almighty dollar. The money that you may lose (or potentially gain!) by taking on a campaign for public office. Lose money? Whatever do we mean? Well, you may need to take time off from your job. You may need to dip into your savings. You may need to spend money on yourself. The hope is that these investments will pay off with a new career that may make you more money and allow you more free time and more freedom in general. But we don't want to throw your financial health into jeopardy! So let's take an accurate account of what you are earning, where you can save or cut back to support yourself during a campaign, and what your future income might look like.

In order to do that, we will need to figure out a few things, such as your expenses, your savings, your debt, and if applicable, your income and/or your partner's income. **Monika** will illustrate how to do this in just four steps that are neither easy nor insurmountable!

STEP ONE: Monika writes down her monthly expenses.

MONIKA'S MONTHLY EXPENSES	
EXPENSE	**AMOUNT**
Rent and Utilities	$765
Transportation	$100
Health Insurance	$264
Cell Phone Bill	$115
Entertainment	$200
Food	$300
Gym	$80
Miscellaneous/Unexpected Expenses	$100
Debt Payments	$300
Total Expenses Per Month	$2,224

STEP TWO: Monika tallies her monthly income.

★ Minimum wage ($7.25 an hour) at the local coffee shop: $1,106

★ Driving for a ride-share company and babysitting: approximately $2,000

Total Income: $3,106

STEP THREE: Monika charts a financial plan to make her run possible. When she did her time analysis, she realized she needed to change her hours at the coffee shop and cut back on driving—which means a significant income reduction. So, she needs to be creative in figuring out how to drastically slash her monthly expenses.

MONIKA

I'm sure if I asked a financial planner what they thought about me running for office, they would tell me not to do it. I mean, I'm a car accident or family illness away from a scary place financially. Although I suppose I always have my parents as a safety net, I still feel this isn't a sound financial decision. Is this where I throw in the towel?

STEP FOUR: Monika considers the salary she'd earn once elected and what her financial forecast would look like then.

Let's look at the financial plan Monika charted out to make her run possible.

MONIKA'S PLAN			
CURRENT FINANCES	**MONEY NEEDED**	**FINANCIAL ACTION PLAN**	**FUTURE FINANCIAL FORECAST**
Monika currently earns minimum wage ($7.25 an hour), which brings in $1,106 a month, and earns approximately $2,000 a month from other jobs (driving for a ride-share company, babysitting). Her monthly expenses total $2,224. She has $3,000 in savings.	Because her hours at the coffee shop will be cut in half, she also needs to cut her expenses. She also sells her car for $5,000, which helps pad her savings.	Monika moves home with her parents to eliminate her housing costs and suspends her monthly gym membership. She can use her parents' car to cut transportation costs. Her food costs will also shrink, because she is living at home and eating her mom's famous chicken mole.	Median annual salary for Houston City Council members: $62,983. Monika may get a significant raise!

MONIKA

Okay, this is feeling less risky. Money can seem so abstract and frightening. It was really great to see all this on paper.

I'M A MINIMUM-WAGE WORKER, HOW THE HELL AM I GOING TO DO THIS?

For women working in underpaid or unpaid labor, or who have multiple jobs or third shifts, it may sound crazy to consider making time for a campaign—especially if you don't have control over your own schedule. There are no two ways about it. Having a schedule where you are working to make ends meet can make it much more challenging to run for office. Some would argue it could make it impossible. But we would also argue that your voices are invaluable and ones that must be heard in our government. And! There are experts who can help you navigate this very real challenge. Chapter Fourteen: THE HOLY BIBLE will direct you to organizations with talented political professionals ready to work with you.

At any point in life, leaving one's source of income, for any amount of time, can be scary. Here's what **Heather** had to say after assessing how her finances would be impacted by her run for Congress.

HEATHER

I definitely don't want to take a big financial risk, especially as I head into the later years of my life, when I will be living off my retirement savings. But because my husband and I both work and have been able to save some money, and because I negotiated with my union so my nursing job is secure if I don't win my campaign, I am confident I can take on the financial risk of running for office.

Here's what **Shawnta** decided after completing the steps.

SHAWNTA

Because I'm not leaving my full-time job and income, I'm feeling okay about running. But I also know that there are costs that will definitely add up (childcare, housekeeping, etc.), so I've decided to rent out my beach house for the year for some extra income.

Could you rent a room in your place for extra income? Is moving in with a parent, friend, or child and cutting your rent or mortgage altogether an option, like it was for Monika?

All of these women have very specific financial situations that may or may not reflect yours. We share them not to prescribe financial decisions, but rather we hope that they'll reveal possibilities—ways you could cut expenses and/or invest some of your own money into your run for office.

Your finances are an area where it's wise to get good advice. Make a date to go over your plan with your friend Dana, who also happens to be a financial advisor/budget guru. Hopefully, you already identified Dana on your Campaign Supporter List, right?! But for now, let's devise the plan ourselves!

STEP ONE: Do an inventory of your monthly expenses.

EXPENSE	AMOUNT	EXPENSE	AMOUNT
Rent/Mortgage		Credit Card Payments	
Health Insurance		Other Debt Payments	
Utilities		Clothing	
Food		Entertainment	
Transportation		Charity/Donations	
Auto Insurance		Grooming	
Auto Loan		Child Support/Alimony	
Student Loan Payment		Other Expenses	
Childcare		**Total**	

STEP TWO:

What is your monthly income? _____

Do you have savings you could draw from, if needed? _____

If you are losing income or increasing your personal expenses to make a campaign happen, how much is the minimum you need to live on? _____

STEP THREE: It's time to chart your financial plan. If yours doesn't require you to lose any income or make any changes that affect your finances, then off you go to the next chapter. But if you need to dip into savings and/or take time off from work to fund your campaign, then let's chart a plan.

Where can you save? _____
_____
_____
_____

Are there things you could temporarily suspend or cut out (gym membership, mani-pedis)? _____
_____
_____
_____

Are there services you are paying for that you could potentially enlist volunteers (hello, Campaign Supporter List) to help you with while you campaign (think lawn care, pet care, personal grooming)? _____
_____
_____
_____

If someone is volunteering a service to your campaign that you would normally pay for, be mindful that for federal races, there are campaign finance rules you need to follow. As long as the volunteer is not compensated by anyone else for the service they are providing you, the volunteer does not have to report their help as a contribution to your campaign. For example, you can ask your neighbor to volunteer to walk your dog while you knock on doors as long as your neighbor doesn't run a dog-walking business and is walking your St. Bernard for free. Running in state or local races but want a friend to help with household chores once a week? Check your state's campaign finance rules on volunteers and in-kind contributions.

Again, is subleasing your place possible? Could you talk to your landlord about deferring rent? Who knows, they might be super supportive of your campaign for office! It never hurts to ask. But again, take Kate's advice and know the campaign finance laws that apply to your race before accepting any in-kind contributions.

STEP FOUR: If (sorry, *when!*) you win the election, what will your financial future look like in office? (Will you be taking a pay cut or getting a salary increase?)

Ways my income will change: _____
_____
_____
_____

Use the chart below to map out your ideas and put your plans into action!

————————————'S PLAN			
(Your Name Here)			
CURRENT FINANCES	**MONEY NEEDED**	**FINANCIAL ACTION PLAN**	**FUTURE FINANCIAL FORECAST**

If staring at these numbers makes you feel fortified and ready to attack your campaign, fantastic! If you are daunted by your monthly credit card bills and the harsh reality of not being able to take off any time from work to run for office, we get it. But we want to remind you: money is a big barrier that keeps out people who need to be represented.

Crisanta Duran, Former Colorado State Speaker of the House

You know, if we want more women running for office, we have to look at how we can build support systems that help them, especially if they are going to be making less money by going into public service. We have to address the real challenges women face when they're thinking about whether they're going to be able to run and succeed in their real lives.

Financial barriers are the reason why our government is run by mostly older, white, wealthy men. They have the time, the money, and the access to more money to run for office. Put another way, they have the luxury of leading. It's time to take that luxury back.

In addition to your financial friend who will check your math, you will also be, soon enough, at the holy grail of chapters . . . Chapter Fourteen: THE HOLY BIBLE. After we look at your whole life (we still have career and care coming right up!), we are going to address a big piece of the puzzle: the amazing organizations that can support your run. Organizations that know exactly why women have less access to wealth and that work to combat the barriers they face.

You just got through a deep analysis of your time and money. Now, check off some damn boxes.

KEEP READING. STAY WORKING.

We need you.

I'm Running for Office.

❮ THE CHECKLIST ❯

1. I know why it's IMPERATIVE that more women run for office. ❑

2. I was nominated by _____.

3. Oh, hell yes, I'm qualified to run for office. ❑

4. I'm running for office to _____.

5. The office I'm running for is _____.

6. The filing deadlines for this office are _____.

7. The other requirements for this office are _____.

8. I have met those requirements. ❑

9. I've told these lucky people I'm going to run for office, because making this promise to myself and others matters: _____.

10. I've completed my week of self-promotion. ❑

11. I've built my Campaign Supporter List in a good ol'-fashioned spreadsheet. ❑

12. My fundraising goal is $_____.

13. I've done a full inventory of my online presence and set my damn privacy settings. ❑

14. When asked about any potentially problematic items found about me online, I'm going to respond by saying: _____.

15. I absolutely know what I'm going to wear as a candidate. ❑

16. **I've found the time to run for office. ❑**

17. **I've stared at the numbers and have figured out my financial plan to run for office. ❑**

> *You've thought about time and money. What other aspects of life do you need to consider?*

JUNE

KATE

She Believed She Could, SO SHE DID

Nancy Pelosi

Nancy Pelosi grew up in a political family. Her father served as mayor of Baltimore and represented the city in Congress. Nancy's brother also later served as mayor of Baltimore. The family home was a hotbed of political activity; the first floor was converted into a constituent office for her father, with each of the family's six children manning the desk in two-hour shifts. When she was thirteen, she took over the office altogether.

After college, she and her husband, Paul, moved to San Francisco, where she raised five children and began a booming political career. (That wasn't a typo. FIVE. CHILDREN.) She started a Democratic party club in her home. She was the Chair of the California Democratic Party, where she honed her skills for recruiting candidates and raising money. Then she decided to run for office herself. In 1987 she was sworn in as a member of Congress.

Representing San Francisco in Congress, she fought for AIDS funding when no one else would. She passed a new GI bill for veterans of wars in Iraq and Afghanistan. She ensured that women's health was front and center in the Affordable Care Act. When she became the first female Speaker of the House in American history, she took the gavel and made some changes. In the first 100 hours of her speakership, she raised the minimum wage, enacted the 9/11 commission report, and ended tax subsidies for oil companies.

She doesn't drink coffee—she prefers hot water with lemon. She rarely sleeps. She works at all hours. She's raised hundreds of millions of dollars for candidates. She says, "I don't do downtime." She signs her text messages to other members of Congress, "–Nancy." She filibustered on the House floor for eight hours in four-inch heels to protect DREAMers. She's encouraged countless women to run. She knows you can't be "the first" if you're also "the only." She's Nancy Fucking Pelosi.

"I felt compelled to run. I had never run for office before. It was a six-way primary: myself and five men. I don't think people thought I was going to win. I wasn't an Ivy League–educated lawyer, for one thing. But I had experience in government and I had heart and I had faith. My life changed, and I realized I had nothing to lose and everything to give."

—CONGRESSWOMAN LISA BLUNT ROCHESTER
(D–DE)

Chapter Thirteen

BUT SERIOUSLY, HOW WILL THIS WORK IN MY REAL LIFE?

PART DEUX

How Will This Work with Your Job?

★

The Care You Give, the Care You Need

HOW WILL THIS WORK WITH MY JOB/WORK/ CAREER?

We may have figured out some pieces of making this dream run a reality, but if you can't take a leave of absence from your job, how will you find the time or money? Or what if your job doesn't allow you to run for office? What then?

So much of our time and identity is wrapped up in what we do to make money. One of the first questions we're often asked when meeting someone new is "What do you do?" It's how we size people up and how we feel like we're getting ahead. It's how many of us self-identify and how we spend most of our days.

So, what to do about work and running for office?

Choosing to run for office is the same as deciding to interview for a new job. There's a risk you might not get the position, in which case you can go back to your current job, if they will have you back. But there's also a potentially huge reward: another job! And potentially (depending on where you are running), a job where you can continue to do your current job! It's a bit of a gamble, but running for office to become an elected official is one that definitely could pay off, not just for you, but for your entire community.

TALKING TO YOUR EMPLOYER ABOUT YOUR CAMPAIGN

If you are thinking of running for office and need to either cut down on your hours or take a leave of absence, talk to your boss! An employer may love the idea of having an employee on city council and support your venture in general. But be prepared for that not to be the case; your employer might not be thrilled about you scaling back your hours or asking for time off. Plan for the conversation in advance. Have your talking points ready and make your case for what you need. If they can't give it to you, have a response at the ready—even if that response is that you need to take time to consider what they are willing, or unwilling, to do to help you meet your long-term goals.

Here are a few not-so-easy steps for figuring out how a run for office will impact your job or career.

STEP ONE: Requirements. Make sure that your current job doesn't prohibit you from running for office. Unclear on what we mean? Flip back to page 64 and make sure you meet all the requirements to run.

Because I'm no longer on active duty with the military, I am cleared to run for political office. Remember when I said I was going to check in with my friend who works at the Department of Defense about being a veteran and running for office? I did, and I'm good.

STEP TWO: Career Assessment. Do you have to leave your job to run for office? Can you work and run at the same time? Go back to your time log analysis and look at the hours you need to spend as a candidate and elected official to figure this out.

STEP THREE: Career Plan of Action. Chart out a plan of action for your career and consider how your campaign will impact it. Does your career assessment suggest you have to leave your job, ask for time off, or reduce your hours? Or is your race local enough that you can keep working? It's time to put pen to paper and figure out your next move.

STEP FOUR: Future Career Forecast. Ask yourself: could winning your seat lead to future job opportunities or political aspirations?

BETH

I thought I was done working, but running for office feels like a second wind, a new path, an exciting next step. Who knows what doors it will open up?!

Perhaps your years of experience and wisdom in your field have been leading to this moment? Perhaps this is where all your experiences were meant to take you? Perhaps your retirement career is a career in public office?

Let's see what **Monika** came up with after taking these steps. But first a little context: Monika hasn't had the opportunity to pursue her career goals in a

---

DO YOU NEED A COLLEGE DEGREE TO RUN FOR OFFICE?

Think Monika can't, shouldn't, or maybe isn't really qualified to run for office because she hasn't graduated from college? Well, let us enlighten you: you don't need a college degree to run for office. In fact, there are countless examples of elected officials who don't have a bachelor's degree. For starters, in the 115th Congress, eighteen members have no educational degree beyond a high school diploma and eight members have an associate's degree. Former governor Scott Walker (R-WI) ran for president in 2016 and does not have a college degree. Governor Gary Herbert (R-UT) does not have a college degree. We say go for it, Monika.

meaningful way because she has had to support herself since graduating from high school. At the time, her mother was struggling to find work, and Monika had to take on multiple jobs. When her girlfriend told her their city council seat was open, Monika realized she could actually make her activism join her professional work. Then the idea of running for office superseded her initial plan to save up enough money for college and law school.

MONIKA'S CAREER INVENTORY			
CURRENT JOB	**CAREER ASSESSMENT**	**CAREER PLAN OF ACTION**	**FUTURE CAREER FORECAST**
Monika has several jobs, but no career. After graduating from high school, she intended to go to community college and eventually law school, but she has been living paycheck to paycheck without a break.	Because Monika hasn't been actively pursuing a professional career, she has nothing to give up. She is only gaining career momentum, not losing any.	Being a city councilwoman makes for a great college admissions essay. She has cut back her hours at the coffee shop but is spending eight hours a week babysitting her younger siblings. She's cut back her hours driving for a ride-sharing company, but still takes a shift or two when she can.	As a city councilwoman, Monika wants to advocate for her community and pass smart laws that help those in need. Eventually, she wants to become an immigration attorney. Being a city councilwoman will afford her more time and money and allow her to pursue her higher education.

MONIKA

The idea of serving in public office as a career stepping-stone had never occurred to me! But it makes total sense. I'm so excited to have put a plan together to make this all happen.

A move toward public office could be exactly the right one if you need a push toward your professional passion. If you haven't been actively making steps toward pursuing your career, why not let public office be that step? Why the eff not?

Monika's foray into politics could very well be an incredible launch into an exciting professional life. It won't be easy. Monika has to carefully manage her finances and make many personal sacrifices to make it happen. But Monika will also be engaging some very important organizations in, you guessed it, Chapter Fourteen: THE HOLY BIBLE!

I always get pissed when people say, "Are you a stay-at-home mom, or do you work?" Um . . . staying at home and raising my children is way harder than the interior design career I had pre-kids. I think mothering is a beautiful career that's undervalued. To me, sitting on a school board seat would simply be an extension of that.

The way women decide to define the words "career" and "job" and their motherhood is entirely up to them.

Liz Brown, Columbus City Councilwoman

When my opportunity came, I was seven months pregnant with my first baby and Election Day was eighty-five days away. I was concerned about how I could work brand-new motherhood into the mix of get-out-the-vote efforts, Election Day, and then—here's hoping—actually serving on city council. I overcame those doubts by consulting with my family, and especially my husband, who told me he'd be mad if I didn't run—for many reasons, but especially because he knew I badly wanted to. And what else could make our soon-to-be daughter prouder?

Now let's put the steps we outlined into practice and figure out how *your* career or job might be affected by a run for office.

STEP ONE: Requirements.

> Does your current job prohibit you from running for office? ❑ No! ❑ Yes. If yes, what will you do about that? _____
>
> _____
>
> _____

STEP TWO: Career Assessment. Check your time log analysis from the previous chapter.

> Do you need to take time off from work to run? _____
>
> _____
>
> _____

STEP THREE: Career Plan of Action.

How would you have to alter your current career to run for office (take a leave of absence, reduce your hours, or protect your job for after your campaign)? _____

STEP FOUR: Future Career Forecast.

Could winning your seat open up future job opportunities or political aspirations? What might these be? _____

Again, no matter where you are on your career track, a run for and holding an elected office will most likely always make an impressive statement on your résumé.

Now that we've examined the intersection of our work and our run, let's look at . . .

THE CARE YOU GIVE, THE CARE YOU NEED

Plain and simple: women are the majority of caregivers in the United States. Data shows that, yes, more men are sharing in caregiving than in the past, but women still represent 75 percent of all caregivers. On average, women spend 21.9 hours a week providing care to others. For some women, it's a joy, and for others, it's a daily challenge. For many, it's something in between. We want to acknowledge the care you give so that we can figure out how it fits in to your run for office.

Just as important is the care you need. We want to acknowledge and create space for the self-care you require in your run for office. This could be anything from quiet time with a favorite book to exercise to meditation to therapy to time with friends to getting a mani-pedi. Women often put themselves at the bottom of the list of people to take care of.

MONIKA

I've never used the term "self-care" in my life and really had to think about what the hell it meant. I do feel a whole lot more focused and emotionally stable when I meditate. I've never prioritized it before, but I will now!

BETH

Running is a newfound passion of mine—did I mention I just completed a marathon? I want to protect my runs as I campaign. It might mean waking up when the sun rises, but if that's what it takes, I'll do it.

You are most likely *already* stretched thin in your life, and as a candidate, the pressures on you will definitely mount. You'll face new challenges, new pulls on your time, new stressors, and new scrutiny. We urge you to truly think about the things you need to make yourself feel whole, mentally safe, and ready to face anything. Get ready to step. It. Up.

STEP ONE: Inventory the care you give and the care you need.

STEP TWO: Decide (depending on your time log analysis) what you can let go of and what is nonnegotiable.

STEP THREE: Chart a plan of action that fulfills your needs.

STEP FOUR: Consider how your caretaking and self-care needs might change once you're elected.

Before you dive in, let's take a look at **Hilda's** situation. Caregiving is a huge part of Hilda's identity as a mother, as well as a part of her campaign story. Here's Hilda's game plan.

HILDA

At first, I was completely freaked out about the idea of asking anyone for help. But once I started, I found people's responses to my requests . . . well, they almost brought me to tears. So many of my friends and family members jumped at the chance to help me. As I would for them, of course. It truly takes a village. And my plan engages my amazing village. It feels really good.

HILDA'S CARE INVENTORY			
CURRENT CARE GIVEN AND NEEDED	**HOW A CAMPAIGN WILL IMPACT HER CARE**	**CARE PLAN OF ACTION**	**FUTURE CARE FORECAST**
Hilda does 90 percent of the caretaking for her family. Her husband does the rest. Hilda knows she needs to spend more time on self-care. She tries to paint in her home studio when she can, but it's always the first thing she lets go. She is going to prioritize making the time to paint to keep her mentally sound.	Even though Hilda is safeguarding important family time, she still has to figure out how to hand over some care hours to others. She must ask for and accept help.	Because her family is reliant on her husband to bring in 100 percent of the income while she runs, Hilda asks her sister to move in and help care for the kids. She also asks her friends to commit to a weekly meal plan where they cook and bring over dinners for her family and to help with laundry. She carves out an hour in her schedule once a week to paint.	If elected, she will hire a caretaker for her kids and her sister will move back out.

Hilda set firm boundaries on her campaign hours to safeguard time with her kids, but she still needs help. Taking care of children is a full-time job, and enlisting support for the unforeseen circumstances that are family life (one child is home sick, another child left their lunchbox at home) is necessary for Hilda. She makes use of her campaign support list to help pick up the slack.

Because **Heather**, like so many women, is also taking care of an elderly parent, this exercise is incredibly important to making a campaign work in her real life. Here's what she had to say after completing her inventory.

HEATHER

As a nurse I always think I'm the only one who can appropriately take care of anyone else. I realize, though, that I need to outsource the care of my mother-in-law that I've been responsible for. I'm going to ask my brother-in-law to care for her during the week and my newly retired RN friend to care for her on the weekends. I also know that if (and when!) I'm elected, I'll be able to hire a full-time aide so my mother-in-law can enjoy the consistency of one caregiver.

Shawnta has to make time for the care she provides her daughter and her elderly mother, but she also needs to prioritize the self-care of her sobriety.

SHAWNTA

After going through the steps in this chapter I know that none of this is possible if I don't carve out time for my AA meetings. There is no campaign and no life without them. This is my main priority, and everything else (money, time, career) falls behind that.

Again, the only one who can decide what your priorities are . . . is you. So let's get serious about figuring out how much care you give and receive and then figure out what you can outsource during your campaign and what you must safeguard.

STEP ONE: Inventory the care you give and the care you need.

How many hours of care do you give each week? _____

What self-care do you need each week to be at your best? _____

_____

_____

RE-CENTERING MOTHERHOOD IN YOUR CAMPAIGN

The same way having access to wealth disproportionately keeps everyone out of politics save for older white men, primary caregiving does the same. For so long, women were more likely to run for office after their children were grown and out on their own. For many women, raising kids and considering a campaign for office seems out of reach and unthinkable. Many women might ask themselves, "Why not wait until the kids are out of the house and not financially dependent?" How could a woman with small children—who in all likelihood is already paid less for doing equal work, has less accumulated wealth, and has fewer powerful networks to tap into—*also* consider running for office when the cost of childcare could be more than she pays in rent?

There is some good news for the huge pool of mothers who can't imagine taking on a run while being primary caregivers. In 2018, the Federal Election Commission unanimously approved a petition filed by New York congressional candidate Liuba Grechen Shirley requesting that the childcare expenses she incurred while campaigning for office be a legitimate campaign expense. Hillary Clinton, more than two dozen members of Congress, and advocacy groups filed letters in support of her request. Because of the FEC's approval, candidates—men or women—can use campaign funds to pay for childcare expenses. Hopefully, this will encourage many more mothers to add their voices to the policy-making process.

STEP TWO: Decide what you can let go of and what is nonnegotiable. Refer back to your time analysis to do some soul searching on the amount of time devoted to caregiving.

How many hours of caregiving (if any) can you free up for your campaign? _____

_____

_____

Reminder: You *can* safeguard your care hours, and in fact, you can make that safeguarding and protecting a part of your story as a woman candidate running for office, if you choose.

What self-care must you make time for? _____

_____

_____

_____

What self-care can you afford to lose? _____

_____

_____

_____

STEP THREE: Chart a plan of action that fulfills your needs.

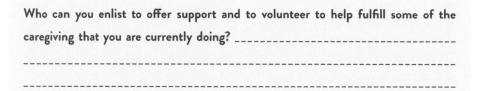

Who can you enlist to offer support and to volunteer to help fulfill some of the caregiving that you are currently doing? _____

_____

_____

Who can you enlist to help you out so that you can safeguard and prioritize needed self-care? _____

_____

_____

STEP FOUR: Look ahead: Consider how your caregiving and self-care needs might change once you are elected.

> Will the office you're running for provide you with more money and/or time, or less? How will this affect your caregiving and self-care? _____
>
> _____
>
> _____
>
> _____

Do you never want to read the word "care" again? If so, we are with you! Hopefully you have a plan that will allow you to preserve the activities that are most important to you while still freeing up time for a campaign.

If you've been reading this last chapter with a look of sheer terror on your face as you think, "There is no way in hell I have the time and money to do this!" or "My career won't support this run and I take care of too many people to make it happen!" or maybe "Is there another book on this same subject I can read? Because these ladies SUCK."

To you we reply, "Wow. That's a lot of feedback. And please stop screaming at us." And then we say . . . there is really good news ahead.

Chapter Fourteen: THE HOLY BIBLE, which we've referenced about a million times, is just around the corner. There are organizations created specifically to help you fill in the gaps. We have taken you through how this run will work in your real life, and these organizations are going to support you even further. They are the next step in this process. It's time to read the bible. And it's just a few pages away!

KEEP READING. STAY WORKING.

We need you.

I'm Running for Office.

THE CHECKLIST

1. I know why it's IMPERATIVE that more women run for office. ❑

2. I was nominated by _____.

3. Oh, hell yes, I'm qualified to run for office. ❑

4. I'm running for office to _____.

5. The office I'm running for is _____.

6. The filing deadlines for this office are _____.

7. The other requirements for this office are _____.

8. I have met those requirements. ❑

9. I've told these lucky people I'm going to run for office, because making this promise to myself and others matters: _____.

10. I've completed my week of self-promotion. ❑

11. I've built my Campaign Supporter List in a good ol'-fashioned spreadsheet. ❑

12. My fundraising goal is $_____.

13. I've done a full inventory of my online presence and set my damn privacy settings. ❑

14. When asked about any items found online about me (photos, arrests, etc.), I'm going to respond by saying: _____.

15. I absolutely know what I'm going to wear as a candidate. ❑

16. I've found the time to run for office. ❑

17. I've stared at the numbers and have figured out my financial plan to run for office. ❑

18. **I understand how a run will impact my career.** ❑

19. **I have inventoried my self-care and caregiving, and I know how each will be sacrificed or safeguarded in my run.** ❑

JUNE

KATE

Use this space to simply doodle.

She Believed She Could, **SO SHE DID**

Mazie Hirono

When she was seven years old, Mazie, her mother, and her younger brother traveled by ship in steerage from Japan to Hawaii, seeking a better life. Once there, they shared one room in a boarding house while her mother worked multiple low-wage jobs.

Mazie worked in the school cafeteria and delivered newspapers to earn money for her family. With her savings and the help of student loans, she attended college and law school. She worked as a legislative aide, a private practicing attorney, and on political campaigns before running for office herself.

She served in the Hawaii State House of Representatives and was elected lieutenant governor before she decided to run for Congress in 2006. After serving in the House for three terms, she ran for the Senate. In 2012, she was elected and became the first Asian American woman, the only Buddhist, and the only immigrant in the Senate.

When the Senate was debating health care reform, Mazie focused on the human side of health care policy, sharing that her sister died from pneumonia because her parents could not afford her care. Fighting back tears, Mazie said, "She died at home, not in a hospital where she could have been saved." During the debate, she said having health insurance allowed her to focus on her job and career. "Now here I am a United States senator, I am fighting kidney cancer, and I am just so grateful that I had health insurance so that I could concentrate on the care I needed rather than how the heck I was going to afford the care that was going to probably save my life."

"Being here in Congress is not as hard as it was to get here."

———

—CONGRESSWOMAN BRENDA LAWRENCE (D-MI)

THE HOLY BIBLE

Take Advantage of the
Resources Available to You

The reason we refer to this chapter over and over throughout the book as THE HOLY BIBLE is because you can turn to it for support and guidance in times of sorrow and doubt! You have done so much work so far on narrowing down where you want to run and why, and you've prepared yourself as much as possible for a run that fits into your real life.

And now it's time for the reinforcements to arrive. Ladies, we're calling for backup!

THE CAVALRY IS COMING!

And by cavalry we mean organizations created specifically to help you run for office, all listed in one spot!

Why is this so important? Because there are systems in place in our country that systematically keep people who don't have money or power out of political life. If you want to change that system, this chapter is for you. If you feel like you've been kept out of political life because of your lack of money or power, this chapter is for you. If you want to run so that you can help people who lack money and power, then sweetheart, this whole book is for you.

Your voice is needed.

Your representation is needed.

There are organizations that have been formed *specifically* to make sure that your voice is heard. There are literally hundreds of these organizations working in towns, cities, states, and across the country trying to elect more women and people like you to office. They are here to support YOU! Yes, you!

There are organizations that provide leadership and campaign training for women running up and down the ballot. Some provide direct financial support to candidates. Others coach you on how to raise money, give recommendations on building your budget, or even help you find talented people to run your campaign. If you've left a chapter of this book thinking, "Wow, I need help with this"—be it fundraising or finding election deadlines or talking to people about your vision— chances are there's an organization out there to help you with your specific challenge.

But how to find many of them in one spot? You are in luck. Take a deep breath and check out the next page.

THE CAVALRY

NATIONAL

Elect Her-Campus Women Win (Nonpartisan)

Emerge America (Democrat)

EMILY's List (Democrat)

Empowered Women (Republican)

Feminist Majority PAC (Nonpartisan)

Higher Heights for America (Nonpartisan)

LPAC (Democrat)

MANA, A National Latina Organization (Nonpartisan)

Modern Republican Women PAC (Republican)

National Congress of Black Women, Inc. (Nonpartisan)

National Federation of Democratic Women (Democrat)

National Federation of Republican Women (Republican)

National Organization for Women (Nonpartisan)

PODER PAC (Nonpartisan)

The Policy Circle (Nonpartisan)

Project GOPink (Republican)

Rachel's Action Network (RAN) (Nonpartisan)

Ready to Lead (Nonpartisan)

Ready to Run National Training Network (Nonpartisan)

Republican Majority for Choice (Republican)

RightNOW Women PAC (Republican)

ROSA PAC (Nonpartisan)

Run for Something (Democrat)

Running Start (Nonpartisan)

She Should Run (Nonpartisan)

Smart Girl Politics (Nonpartisan)

The Susan B. Anthony List Candidate Fund (Republican)

Truman National Security Project (Nonpartisan)

Value in Electing Women Political Action Committee (VIEW PAC) (Republican)

VoteRunLead (Nonpartisan)

Women's Action for New Directions PAC (WAND PAC) (Nonpartisan)

Women's Campaign Fund (Nonpartisan)

Women Under Forty PAC (WUFPAC) (Nonpartisan)

ALABAMA

Alabama Association of University Women (Nonpartisan)

Alabama Federation of Democratic Women (Democrat)

Alabama Federation of Republican Women (Republican)

Alabama NOW (Nonpartisan)

Leadership Alabama (Nonpartisan)

Ready to Run Alabama (Nonpartisan)

ALASKA

Alaska Federation of Republican Women (Republican)

Alaska NOW (Nonpartisan)

Alaska Women for Political Action (Nonpartisan)

Leadership Anchorage (Nonpartisan)

ARIZONA

Arizona Federation of Democratic Women (Democrat)

Arizona Federation of Republican Women (Republican)

Arizona List (Democrat)

Arizona Women's Political Caucus PAC (Nonpartisan)

The Dodie Londen Excellence in Public Service Series (Republican)

Emerge Arizona (Democrat)

ARKANSAS

Arkansas Federation of Democratic Women (Democrat)

Arkansas Federation of Republican Women (Republican)

Arkansas GOP Campaign Training (Republican)

Arkansas NOW (Nonpartisan)

Campaign Management Training Seminar (Nonpartisan)

Leadership Arkansas (Nonpartisan)

Women Lead Arkansas (Nonpartisan)

CALIFORNIA

Black Women Organized for Political Action (Nonpartisan)

California Federation of Democratic Women (Democrat)

California Federation of Republican Women (Republican)

California Women Lead (Nonpartisan)

California Women's Leadership Association PAC (Republican)

California Women's List (Democrat)

The Center for Asian Pacific American Women (Nonpartisan)

Close the Gap CA (Nonpartisan)

Emerge California (Democrat)

IGNITE (Nonpartisan)

Latinas Lead California (Nonpartisan)

Los Angeles African American Women PAC (Democrat)

New Leaders Council Los Angeles (Nonpartisan)

Ready to Run California (Nonpartisan)

COLORADO

Colorado 50/50 (Nonpartisan)

Colorado BlueFlower Fund (Democrat)

Colorado Federation of Republican Women (Republican)

Colorado Springs Leadership Institute (Nonpartisan)

Leadership Denver (Nonpartisan)

CONNECTICUT

Connecticut Federation of Democratic Women (Democrat)

Connecticut Federation of Republican Women (Republican)

Connecticut NOW (Nonpartisan)

Ready to Run Connecticut (Nonpartisan)

Women's Campaign School at Yale University (Nonpartisan)

DELAWARE

Delaware Federation of Republican Women (Republican)

Delaware NOW (Nonpartisan)

Leadership Delaware (Nonpartisan)

Women's Democratic Club of Delaware PAC (Democrat)

DISTRICT OF COLUMBIA

New Leaders Council Washington, DC (Nonpartisan)

WeLEAD (Nonpartisan)

WIN (Democrat)

FLORIDA

Florida Women's Political Caucus PAC (Nonpartisan)

Florida Women's Political Network (Republican)

Maggie's List (Republican)

Ruth's List (Democrat)

The Tillie Fowler Series (Republican)

GEORGIA

Georgia Federation of Democratic Women (Democrat)

Georgia Federation of Republican Women (Republican)

Georgia Women's Policy Institute
(Nonpartisan)

Georgia's WIN List (Democrat)

Her Term (Democrat)

NewPower PAC (Nonpartisan)

HAWAII

Patsy T. Mink PAC (Democrat)

Ready to Run Hawaii (Nonpartisan)

IDAHO

Gracie's List (Nonpartisan)

Idaho Federation of Republican Women
(Republican)

Idaho NOW (Nonpartisan)

Ready to Lead (Nonpartisan)

ILLINOIS

Illinois Democratic Women (Democrat)

Illinois Federation of Republican Women
(Republican)

The Illinois Lincoln Series (Republican)

Illinois Women's Institute for Leadership
(Democrat)

New Leaders Council Chicago (Nonpartisan)

Ready to Run Illinois (Nonpartisan)

INDIANA

Democratic Women's Caucus (Democrat)

Indiana Federation of Republican Women
(Republican)

Indiana Leadership Association (Nonpartisan)

Ready to Run Indiana (Nonpartisan)

The Richard G. Lugar Excellence in Public
Service Series (Republican)

The Stanley K. Lacy Executive Leadership
Series (Nonpartisan)

IOWA

50-50 in 2020 (Nonpartisan)

Carrie Chapman Catt Center for Women and
Politics (Nonpartisan)

DAWN's List (Democrat)

Iowa N.E.W. Leadership (Nonpartisan)

PURSE (People United for Republican Sisters'
Elections) PAC (Republican)

KANSAS

The Dwight D. Eisenhower Series (Republican)

Kansas Advancing Women (Nonpartisan)

Kansas Federation of Democratic Women's
Clubs (Democrat)

Kansas Federation of Republican Women
(Republican)

Kansas Leadership Center Programs
(Nonpartisan)

KENTUCKY

Emerge Kentucky (Democrat)

Kentucky Republican Women's Roundtable
(Republican)

Kentucky Women's Political Caucus
(Nonpartisan)

Women Leading Kentucky (Nonpartisan)

LOUISIANA

Louisiana Center for Women and Government
(Nonpartisan)

Louisiana Federation of Republican Women
(Republican)

New Leaders Council Louisiana (Nonpartisan)

The New Orleans Regional Leadership Institute
(Nonpartisan)

Ready to Run Louisiana (Nonpartisan)

MAINE

Emerge Maine (Democrat)

Institute for Civic Leadership (Nonpartisan)

Maine Federation of Republican Women
(Republican)

Maine Women's Policy Center (Nonpartisan)

MARYLAND

Emerge Maryland (Democrat)

The LEADERship (Nonpartisan)

Leadership Maryland (Nonpartisan)

Maryland Federation of Republican Women
(Republican)

Republican Campaign Training School
(Republican)

United Democratic Women of Maryland
(Democrat)

MASSACHUSETTS

Emerge Massachusetts (Democrat)

Massachusetts Women's Political Caucus
(Nonpartisan)

MassGAP (Nonpartisan)

Women's Pipeline for Change (Nonpartisan)

MICHIGAN

Emerge Michigan (Democrat)

MI List (Democrat)

Michigan Political Leadership Program
(Nonpartisan)

The Michigan Series (Republican)

Republican Women's Federation of Michigan
(Republican)

MINNESOTA

Frontrunners: Women with Political Ambition
(Nonpartisan)

The Minnesota Series (Republican)

University of Minnesota Center on Women
and Public Policy (Nonpartisan)

VOICES of Conservative Women Political
Action Committee (VOICESPAC)
(Republican)

Women Candidate Development Coalition
(Nonpartisan)

Women Winning Minnesota (Nonpartisan)

MISSISSIPPI

Mississippi Federation of Democratic Women
(Democrat)

Mississippi Federation of Republican Women
(Republican)

Mississippi N.E.W. Leadership (Nonpartisan)

Ready to Run Mississippi (Nonpartisan)

Stennis Institute of Government Campaign
Training (Nonpartisan)

MISSOURI

Missouri Federation of Women's Democratic
Clubs (Democrat)

Missouri NOW (Nonpartisan)

Pipeline to Public Office (Nonpartisan)

The Show Me State Series (Republican)

Sue Shear Institute for Women in Public Life
(Nonpartisan)

MONTANA

Carol's List (Democrat)

Montana Federation of Republican Women
(Republican)

Women's Policy Leadership Institute
(Nonpartisan)

NORTH DAKOTA

NEW Leadership Northern Lights
(Nonpartisan)

Ready to Run North Dakota (Nonpartisan)

Rural Leadership North Dakota (Nonpartisan)

NEBRASKA

ICAN Women's Leadership Conference
(Nonpartisan)

Nebraska Federation of Democratic Women
(Democrat)

Nebraska Federation of Republican Women
(Republican)

Nebraska NOW (Nonpartisan)

NEVADA

Emerge Nevada (Democrat)

Leadership Las Vegas (Nonpartisan)

Nevada Federation of Republican Women
(Republican)

NEW HAMPSHIRE
NEW Leadership New England (Nonpartisan)
The Vesta Roy Series (Republican)

NEW JERSEY
Emerge New Jersey (Democrat)
Lead New Jersey (Nonpartisan)
LUPE Fund Inc. (Nonpartisan)
PAM's List (Democrat)
Ready to Run New Jersey (Nonpartisan)

NEW MEXICO
Emerge New Mexico (Democrat)
Leadership New Mexico (Nonpartisan)
New Mexico Federation of Republican Women
    (Republican)
New Mexico NOW (Nonpartisan)
Ready to Run New Mexico (Nonpartisan)

NEW YORK
The Eleanor Roosevelt Legacy Committee
    (Democrat)
Leadership New York (Nonpartisan)
New York Federation of Republican Women
    (Republican)
WE PAC (Democrat)
WomenElect (Nonpartisan)
Women's Taking Action in Politics (TAP) Fund
    (Nonpartisan)

NORTH CAROLINA
Democratic Women of North Carolina
    (Democrat)
Leadership North Carolina (Nonpartisan)
Lillian's List (Democrat)
NC Women United (Nonpartisan)
North Carolina Federation of Republican
    Women (Republican)

OHIO
The Jo Ann Davidson Ohio Leadership
    Institute (Republican)

Leadership Ohio (Nonpartisan)
Matriots (Nonpartisan)
Ready to Run Ohio (Nonpartisan)
WE Lead (Nonpartisan)
WE Succeed (Nonpartisan)

OKLAHOMA
Oklahoma Federation of Republican Women
    (Republican)
Pipeline to Politics (Nonpartisan)
Sally's List (Nonpartisan)
Women Lead Oklahoma (Nonpartisan)

OREGON
American Association of University Women
    Oregon (Nonpartisan)
Center for Women's Leadership (Nonpartisan)
Emerge Oregon (Democrat)
Oregon Women's Campaign School
    (Nonpartisan)
Women's Investment Network (WIN-PAC)
    (Democrat)

PENNSYLVANIA
The Anne Anstine Excellence in Public Service
    Series (Republican)
Emerge Pennsylvania (Democrat)
Pennsylvania Center for Women and Politics at
    Chatham University (Nonpartisan)
Pennsylvania Rural Leadership Program
    (Nonpartisan)
Represent! PAC (Democrat)
She Can Win (Nonpartisan)
Women for the Future of Pittsburgh
    (Nonpartisan)

RHODE ISLAND
New Leaders Council Rhode Island
    (Nonpartisan)
Rhode Island Democratic Party Women's
    Caucus (Democrat)
Rhode Island Federation of Republican Women
    (Republican)

SOUTH CAROLINA

Pathway to Politics (Nonpartisan)

Political Institute for Women (Nonpartisan)

South Carolina GOP Academy (Republican)

SOUTH DAKOTA

Ready to Run South Dakota (Nonpartisan)

South Dakota Agriculture and Rural Leadership, Inc. (SDARL) (Nonpartisan)

South Dakota Federation of Republican Women (Republican)

TENNESSEE

Emerge Tennessee (Democrat)

Tennessee Federation of Republican Women (Republican)

Women for Tennessee's Future (Democrat)

Women in Numbers PAC (Nonpartisan)

TEXAS

Annie's List (Democrat)

The Latino Center for Leadership Development (Nonpartisan)

Leadership Women (Nonpartisan)

Ready to Run New Mexico/Texas Borderlands (Nonpartisan)

Texas Federation of Republican Women (Republican)

Texas Latina PAC (Democrat)

Texas Leadership Institute (Nonpartisan)

UTAH

Real Women Run (Nonpartisan)

Utah Federation of Republican Women (Republican)

Women's Leadership Institute (Nonpartisan)

VERMONT

Emerge Vermont (Democrat)

Snelling Center Vermont Leadership Institute (Nonpartisan)

VIRGINIA

American Majority (Nonpartisan)

Emerge Virginia (Democrat)

Minority Political Leadership Institute (MPLI) (Nonpartisan)

Republican Party of Virginia Ambassador Program (Republican)

Virginia Federation of Republican Women (Republican)

WASHINGTON

Alene Moris National Education for Women's Leadership (Nonpartisan)

Washington NOW (Nonpartisan)

Washington State Federation of Democratic Women (Democrat)

Youth Native Women's Leadership Academy (Nonpartisan)

WEST VIRGINIA

Ready to Run West Virginia

West Virginia Federation of Democratic Women (Democrat)

West Virginia Federation of Republican Women (Republican)

WISCONSIN

Democratic Leadership Institute (Democrat)

Emerge Wisconsin (Democrat)

VOICESPAC Wisconsin (Republican)

WYOMING

Leap into Leadership (Nonpartisan)

Wyoming L.E.A.D (Nonpartisan)

Did we just use six pages of our book for a list of organizations dedicated to helping women get elected? Oh hell yes, we did. And get this. It's not even the full list! The FULL list was too big! Please head to this link right now: **cawp.rutgers.edu/education/leadership-resources**.

There you will find the Center for American Women and Politics (CAWP) at Rutgers University's compilation of organizations that have been formed to help women like you. Take a look at the list both in the Cavalry section in this book and on CAWP's site. You are going to choose the groups you will reach out to for support today.

When choosing which groups to connect with, first think about your story and your identity. Just like we asked you to match where you want to run with problems you want to solve, think about reaching out to the organizations that are best suited to help you run. For instance, if you want to run for town clerk, reaching out to an organization that is dedicated to electing women to state legislatures and Congress might not be the best fit (keep them in mind for your next campaign, though!). Similarly, if you're getting mailings from the AARP, a group organizing millennial women candidates shouldn't be on at the top of your list. Our point is that there are groups looking to elect women just like you.

Jenny Durkan,
Seattle Mayor

Don't know how to file, raise money, or send a press release? Good news: there's a TON of help! Women can join candidate-training programs run by organizations like EMILY's List, Emerge America, and Run for Something.

Here's how Monika, Heather, Hilda, Shawnta, and Beth found the specific organizations from the CAWP list that would take each of their campaigns to the next level.

MONIKA

I'm a proud lesbian, Latina, first-generation immigrant, and I'm under thirty years old. I'm running for city council in Houston, Texas, and will accept all the help I can get. WHO CAN HELP ME?!

Monika browsed the list and jotted down the groups that looked relevant to her and then did a little research online. Through her reading she found Annie's List, a group that helps elect women running for office in Texas. She also found EMILY's List (neither list has any relation to Angie's List—that's where you find a plumber), which recruits, trains, and elects pro-choice Democratic women like Monika up and down the ballot. Next, she checked out LPAC, which, among other things, works to elect candidates who champion LGBTQ rights. She also plans to contact the Latino Victory Project, which supports increasing Latino representation at all levels of government; MANA, an advocacy organization focusing on fostering Latina leadership; New American Leaders, which encourages first- and second-generation Americans; and Run for Something, an organization dedicated to electing young progressive candidates to local offices.

> *I'm a Native American woman, a nurse, and a Democrat, in that order! I live in North Dakota, and I'm running for Congress. I'd love to contact anyone and everyone who can help me.*

Heather's first step is to contact her tribal leadership about her campaign. She also plans to connect with other tribes who could help get her elected to Congress. Heather's next call is to EMILY's List. She is scheduled to attend their Run to Win training. She also reaches out to the North Dakota Democratic party to let them know she is running for the At-Large congressional seat and to see what resources are available to her. Next, she researches BOLD PAC, which works to elect more diverse candidates to office, and ROSA PAC, which specifically helps elect women of color to Congress. She notes there are new **super PACs** that specifically help elect Native Americans to office, but it is illegal for them to work directly with candidates.

VERY IMPORTANT WORD ALERT PACs and **SUPER PACs**. A political action committee, or PAC, is a political organization formed to raise money to elect or defeat candidates. The federal government limits how much money a PAC can give to a candidate. There are also limits on how much individuals can give to PACs.

A super PAC, on the other hand, is an organization that has no restrictions on how much it can raise or spend in any given election, but they cannot contribute to candidates directly. Instead, a super PAC can make ads and communicate with voters independently of the candidates.

> *I'm an African American woman, a mom, and a registered Democrat. I'm running for a seat on the Los Angeles County Board of Education—and I also love interior design. I'm betting there isn't a group for that?*

There's nothing on her list for design lovers, but for other parts of her identity, **Hilda** will be helped by Higher Heights for America, which is dedicated to building networks and infrastructure to support and increase black women's political power. She plans to also contact Emerge California, an organization that works to train and encourage women to run for local and state offices in California. Two other groups appear on Hilda's list: PowerPAC+, which works to elect progressive candidates of color up and down the ballot, and Leadership LA, which focuses on community issues and leadership development in Los Angeles.

I'm African American and a veteran, I live in Virginia, and I'm running for city council. I have already been leading in my community, but I need help taking my leadership to the next level. Anyone out there?

SHAWNTA

Shawnta scrolls through the list of groups and does some research on her own. Two of the groups on Shawnta's to-do list have already been mentioned: EMILY's List, which works to elect pro-choice Democratic women, and Higher Heights, an organization dedicated to electing black women. She also contacts Emerge Virginia, a group working to train women to run for local and state office in Virginia. She has signed up for the Congressional Black Caucus Institute's Political Boot Camp—a one-week political campaign training program. Shawnta also plans to connect with groups that work to encourage more veterans to run for office, such as VoteVets's Emerging Leaders program and Veterans Campaign training sessions.

I'm running for governor of Iowa and need all the help I can get to make it through a crowded primary and competitive general election.

BETH

To help **Beth** build a competitive campaign to win her primary and general election, she's got a few groups to call. She'll connect with DAWN's List, an Iowa-based group working to support and elect progressive women in the state, and 50-50 in 2020, a bipartisan group working to recruit and mentor women candidates in Iowa. She'll also reach out to Iowa State University's Carrie Chapman Catt Center for Women and Politics, to see what resources, insights, and knowledge they might be able to share with her as she begins her campaign, including a Ready to Run training. On the national side, she'll be calling EMILY's List, which has elected more than a dozen women governors.

Now, you may have noticed that some groups pertain to a number of our candidates and some are specific to individual candidacies. Here are a few things to keep in mind. First, these women are running for different levels of office. Some organizations work to elect candidates only at the federal level, and others focus on state or local elections. And remember that each woman lives in a different state, and political infrastructures to help women get elected vary from state to state. Populous California and Texas have multiple options for Monika and Hilda. But in North Dakota, options for Heather may be more limited.

When looking at what's available to you, bear in mind that the type of seat you're running for, where you're running, and how you identify all intersect. There may not be one group that focuses on all of the different identities you hold. For example, some groups might want to elect young Republican women to Congress. One group might work to elect American Indian women to all offices in New Mexico. And another might want to help women under thirty-five build nonpartisan leadership and networking skills in their cities.

You can narrow your search of the CAWP list by state, by party affiliation, and even by groups that provide campaign training. Go the website right now and do not return to this page until you have least three organizations you will be contacting for support. We will be waiting.

1. _____

2. _____

3. _____

4. _____

5. _____

6. _____

7. _____

Welcome back! What organizations will you contact for help?

GET IN TOUCH WITH THESE ORGANIZATIONS TODAY. Call, text, email, or send them a carrier pigeon letting them know about your candidacy and where you are in your process. Again, they are dedicated to getting you elected. That might mean raising money for you. GREAT! It might mean offering up political advice and advising you on how to run your race. PERFECT! It might mean offering you speaking opportunities at events or in the press. EVEN BETTER! There are talented people looking to help you win. Why leave that help on the sidelines?

Now off you go to change the world! Except for one more teensy-weensy last chapter.

KEEP READING. STAY WORKING.
AND REACH OUT TO THESE GROUPS TODAY.
We need you.

I'm Running for Office.

THE CHECKLIST

1. I know why it's IMPERATIVE that more women run for office. ❑

2. I was nominated by _____.

3. Oh, hell yes, I'm qualified to run for office. ❑

4. I'm running for office to _____.

5. The office I'm running for is _____.

6. The filing deadlines for this office are _____.

7. The other requirements for this office are _____.

8. I have met those requirements. ❑

9. I've told these lucky people I'm going to run for office, because making this promise to myself and others matters: _____.

10. I've completed my week of self-promotion. ❑

11. I've built my Campaign Supporter List in a good ol'-fashioned spreadsheet. ❑

12. My fundraising goal is $_____.

13. I've done a full inventory of my online presence and set my damn privacy settings. ❑

14. When asked about any items found online about me (photos, arrests, etc.), I'm going to respond by saying: _____.

15. I absolutely know what I'm going to wear as a candidate. ❑

16. I've found the time to run for office. ❑

17. I've stared at the numbers and have figured out my finances to run for office. ❑

18. I know how a run will impact my career. ❑

19. I have inventoried my self-care and caregiving, and I know how each will be sacrificed or safeguarded in my run. ❑

20. **The incredible organizations I've contacted for help are** _____
_____
_____.

The New Class

In 2018, a historic number of women ran for office. Here are a few of the glass ceiling–breakers who stepped up and put their names on the ballot— and won. From governors and congresswomen to state leaders and city councilors, these women broke barriers and were the first—but we can bet they won't be the last.

★ **Sharice Davids (D-KS)** is the first lesbian American Indian elected to Congress.

★ **Deb Haaland (D-NM)** joins her as one of the first two American Indian women elected to Congress.

★ **Ilhan Omar (D-MN)** and **Rashida Tlaib (D-MI)** are the first Muslim women elected to Congress.

★ **Ayanna Pressley (D-MA)** is the first African American woman to represent Massachusetts in Congress.

★ **Alexandria Ocasio-Cortez (D-NY)** is the youngest woman, at age 29, to be elected to Congress.

★ **Veronica Escobar (D-TX)**, right, and **Sylvia Garcia (D-TX)** are both the first Latinas to ever represent Texas in Congress.

★ Gun control advocate—mother to Jordan Davis, who was fatally killed by gun violence—and first-time candidate **Lucy McBath (D-GA)** won Georgia's Sixth Congressional district—a seat once held by Newt Gingrich.

SO THEY DID

★ **Marsha Blackburn (R-TN)** is Tennessee's first female senator ever.

★ **Kyrsten Sinema (D-NV)** is the first female senator from Arizona and the first openly bisexual senator in the nation.

★ **Kristi Noem (R-SD)** is the first female governor in South Dakota's history.

★ **Michelle Lujan Grisham (D-NM)** is the first Democratic Latina governor in American history.

★ **Peggy Flanagan (D-MN)**, the new lieutenant governor of Minnesota, is the first woman of color elected to statewide executive office in her state. She's also the second American Indian woman ever elected to a statewide executive office in the country.

★ **Kimberly Yee (R-AZ)**, the newly elected state treasurer, is the first woman of color serving statewide in Arizona.

★ **Letitia James (D-NY)**, New York's new attorney general, is the first woman of color elected statewide in New York.

> "For those of us who have been fortunate enough to achieve some level of success in our own careers, we better darn well help other women, because we've got a long, long way to go. . . . I think it's part of my life's mission to help women succeed and be in positions to help make a difference in our state, our country, and our world."

—CONGRESSWOMAN CHERI BUSTOS (D-IL)

Chapter Fifteen

HOW DO I SUPPORT OTHER WOMEN?

Ask Her to Run

★

Support Her When She Does

★

Interrupt Sexist Bullshit

We are nearing the end, Dear Reader. We've discussed your fears about running. We've outlined how your run will work in your real life. We've even encouraged you to get a new bra. But there is one more step to this process: It's time to support another woman running for office. There are a few ways you can do that.

1. ASK WOMEN TO RUN. Ask other women in your life to run! As you now know, it helps when we ask women to run. It helps even more when we ask them a few times. Who are the women you think would be awesome in office?

WOMAN #1. _____

WOMAN #2. _____

WOMAN #3. _____

WOMAN #4. _____

WOMAN #5. _____

Let's start with the first person on your list. Take her out for a drink or coffee and tell her that you think she should run for office. Explain why you know she'd be great. *Give her a copy of this book.* Tell her that you'll help her with her campaign.

Look back at your list. Are there women of color on your list? If not, consider who you might add. Are there young women on your list? Consider them. Are there mothers on your list? Consider them. Are there LGBTQIA women on your list? Consider them. Are there women who work for hourly wages? Consider them. Are there domestic workers on your list? Consider them. Are there sex workers on your list? Consider them. Are there scientists or engineers on your list? Consider them. Broaden your own lens of not just who should run but who you need to ask, and add them to your list. Consider them. Consider them. Consider them. Consider them.

2. VOTE FOR HER. Voting for women candidates is a fantastic and cost-free way to support women running for office. Not sure about voting for women simply because they are women? Remember these facts from Chapter 1: More women at the table means better outcomes for us all. Women leaders write more legislation, bring more federal money (aka jobs) back to their districts, and are more likely to focus on the issues that are important to women and families. Oh yeah, and they get shit done.

3. DONATE $$$ TO HER CAMPAIGN. As you now well know, campaigns need

HAVE YOU ASKED ANOTHER WOMAN TO RUN FOR OFFICE?

We asked all of the amazing elected women we surveyed, "Have you ever asked another woman to run?" Get inspired by their answers.

Pressley

Yes, of course! And I am thrilled that some of them even said yes. In addition to actively recruiting women to run, I have also actively recruited and trained young women in the disciplines of running campaigns. We must build and diversify both the candidate and the operative benches.

Jayapal

All the time! I believe we stand on the shoulders of others who came before us—Sojourner Truth, Shirley Chisholm, and many others. Our duty is to allow others to stand on our shoulders. I am constantly trying to grow the leadership ladder behind me—it's great to be the first, but I never want to be the last. I have mentored and helped many women to lead and many women to run. It's one of the things I am proudest to have accomplished in my career.

Yes! Easily a dozen.

Brown

Duran

Many times! In the legislature, I worked to open doors for other people, particularly women and people who are from underrepresented communities. I've encouraged them to think about running for office or to get involved with politics in some way. In collaboration with my other colleagues, we've created fellowships in the Capitol to bring in women and people from underrepresented communities so they have the opportunity to see our work firsthand and can get an understanding of how the system works.

Yes, and we need to keep having these conversations! Representation is so crucially important in a field that remains dominated by men. We need to build each other up, even when we don't agree on every single issue. Not only do we owe it to ourselves, but we owe it to every young girl who's watching and learning what the future will have in store for her. We have so much power, and now more than ever, we need to spread that truth.

Evans

Durkan

Yes. And I'm asking YOU to run.

money. When your friend, sister, colleague, neighbor says she is running and she asks you to donate, do it! Even just a little bit—$5 can help pay for that next order of lawn signs. Keep in mind that women candidates of color have less access to financial networks than white candidates and need your campaign contributions even more.

4. DONATE TIME, FOOD, OR SKILLS TO HER CAMPAIGN. In addition to money, campaigns need volunteers to make calls, knock on doors, and train other volunteers. Show up and ask how her campaign needs help. Are you a graphic designer? Offer to help design her campaign materials. Are you great at organizing events? Perhaps you can gather a host committee and spearhead an upcoming fundraiser. Alternatively, you can always send the campaign some pizza! Campaign staffers need fuel, and what is better fuel than carbohydrates covered in cheese, right?!

5. DONATE TIME, FOOD, OR SKILLS TO HER. In front of every woman's campaign is a woman trying to make all the *other* parts of her life work. And behind her is a team of friends and family who can step in and help. In addition to donating your time and energy to her campaign, remember that in the midst of all this, there is a human woman who might need some help. Don't wait to be asked—offer:

★ **Childcare:** Does she need someone to help with childcare or school drop-off and pickup? Offer to watch her children while she speaks at an event or is busy with other campaign activities.

JUNE

Kate, what are overnight oats?

★ **Food:** Organize your friends and develop a meal calendar. Who is bringing their famous taco casserole this week, and who is dropping off overnight oats next week?

★ **Daily Fucking Chores:** We've all got them. They might look different from our houses to yours, but chores exist for everyone. Take a shift, or two, or a week at a time. How good would it feel to come home to a clean house, to learn that the grocery shopping for the week has been done, or to find the laundry folded and dry cleaning picked up?

KATE

If you don't know, you don't deserve to know.

★ **Personal Grooming and Health:** Are you a hairstylist? Make a house call and do her hair. Give her a blowout or braids. Are you the friend who always has perfect done-at-home manicures? Go over and do the candidate's nails. Are you a spin instructor at a studio? Offer women who are running for office one-on-one sessions at off-peak times.

6. INTERRUPT SEXIST AND OPPRESSIVE DIALOGUE AROUND WOMEN RUNNING FOR OFFICE. We've all heard people say things like "I don't know what it is about her. I just don't like her." We may not have known how to respond. But what if we all always responded?

We sent Neelamjit Dhaliwal, a facilitator for the National SEED Project—a program that creates conversational communities to drive personal, organizational, and societal change toward greater equity and diversity—an email asking for her thoughts on the matter. Look what it led to.

FROM: June and Kate

TO: Neelamjit Dhaliwal

SUBJECT: Any help with dis?

Neeti,

I know you've facilitated conversations about equity and diversity for the National SEED Project. Do you have any suggestions for how someone might respond when women candidates are being spoken about in horrifying/sexist/racist terms? We're hoping to include some suggestions on how someone might change or reroute these conversations for our book.

Love you like whoa,
JDR

FROM: Neelamjit Dhaliwal

TO: June and Kate

SUBJECT: Re: Any help with dis?

Hi, Friends,

I'm so happy you are addressing this subject. I grew up in the Sikh faith, often being reminded to stand up for the oppressed and hearing the phrase "Chardi kala." It loosely means maintaining a "positive, buoyant, and optimistic" attitude toward life and the future, particularly in times of darkness. So yes! This is extremely personal for me.

"Interrupting" the oppressive language around women candidates you reference deserves a lot of thought and I'm not sure it's as simple as providing someone with a cheat sheet on how to respond.

What do you have in mind?

—Neelamjit

FROM: June and Kate

TO: Neelamjit Dhaliwal

SUBJECT: Re: Any help with dis?

What exactly do you mean by "interrupt"?

And OOOH A CHEAT SHEET! Can you do that please please please please?

FROM: Neelamjit Dhaliwal

TO: June and Kate

SUBJECT: Re: Any help with dis?

JUNE! I just said I wouldn't provide a simple cheat sheet.

I would, however, tell your reader that we start this work by knowing we all have work to do. At some point in life we've all been in a position of hearing someone say something that we knew to be at odds with our values, but we couldn't find the words to interrupt or engage. Or we've had the experience of realizing, upon reflection, that the words we uttered were rooted in racism, sexism, classism, heterosexism, or cis-sexism.

I'd also add that we must move away from the false binary of either

1. You make oppressive comments, so you are racist/sexist/homophobic/etc.

OR

2. You don't make oppressive comments, so you are not racist/sexist/homophobic/etc.

This work is a daily practice, one which we must learn to sustain and nurture over time.

When I talk about "interrupting" oppressive comments, I don't necessarily mean "to stop a person in the midst of saying something . . ." What I do mean is to cause "a break in the continuity" of a thought process founded in bias. Interrupting is about engaging with people in a way that results in a disruption in their thinking. The purpose is not to silence a person's viewpoint; rather it is to engage it and unpack it.

There are six general principles to follow when one is confronted with oppressive comments.

The Six Principles

1. Ask clarifying questions, like "Can you tell me more? What do you mean when you say she is too ambitious?"

2. Speak from the "I," as in: "I've heard that before, and it made me feel ____."

3. Use data to interrupt. A good example is "Did you know that when women and men in college were asked to estimate their GPA, women underestimated it and men overestimated it?"

4. Invite them to a private conversation with fewer people around to lower the stakes.

5. Acknowledge that they may have been well-intentioned, so focus on impact. Using language like "I realize you may not have meant it this way, but when you said ____, it reinforced ____" can help you and them remain focused on impact.

6. Use humor, but be careful not to shame.

Does this clarify? Again, the work is not as simple as a cheat sheet you can tear out of the book and have with you at all times.

xo
N

FROM: June and Kate

TO: Neelamjit Dhaliwal

SUBJECT: Re: Any help with dis?

Having a tear-out cheat sheet on how to interrupt oppressive language—something you could have with you at all times??!! This is the best idea I've ever heard and we need it.

FROM: Neelamjit DhaliwalL

TO: June and Kate

SUBJECT: Re: Any help with dis?

JUNE DIANE RAPHAEL. You are oversimplifying the work. There are so many principles to put into practice before you just randomly start "interrupting." I would tell your readers to keep in mind the following:

- **Who/Where/When/Why?** Know your audience and where you are when choosing to interrupt. Having a difficult conversation in the privacy of your home with a loved one, for example, is different from interrupting your boss at work. And recognize that it may not always be safe, physically or emotionally, to engage in these conversations.

- **Call in as opposed to calling out.** This is not a time to be "right." This is an opportunity to have a dialogue and create space for movement.

- **Be careful of blaming or shaming.** Try not to judge the person—instead, focus on the statement.

- **Be patient.** The objective is to listen and to engage. Remember that we are always in process.

- **Expect discomfort.** This work is often accompanied by emotionally charged reactions—anger and/or tears are not uncommon, so prepare yourself for a spectrum of experiences.

- **It's never too late.** How do you handle situations when you don't do something in the moment, but want to upon reflection? Give yourself permission to invite the person who made the oppressive comment into a conversation later.

- **Know your bandwidth.** Because these can be difficult and taxing conversations, be aware of your own capacity for engagement.

- **Practice, practice, practice.** If you get it wrong, keep trying. Consider with whom you can share, discuss, or practice the six principles.

FROM: June and Kate

TO: Neelamjit Dhaliwal

SUBJECT: Re: Any help with dis?

These are great and also.

SEND ME THE CHEAT SHEET. NOW.

FROM: Neelamjit Dhaliwal

TO: June and Kate

SUBJECT: Re: Any help with dis?

A white woman expecting a woman of color to do work is PROBLEMATIC, JUNE.

FROM: June and Kate

TO: Neelamjit Dhaliwal

SUBJECT: Re: Any help with dis?

Well, you got me now. Fuck. White woman here in full acknowledgment of asking a woman of color to present this info in a way that this white woman feels is best. I'm sorry and thank you for the interruption. Wish I had a cheat sheet to look at before I had this conversation with you. (KIDDING!)

FROM: Neelamjit Dhaliwal

TO: June and Kate

SUBJECT: Re: Any help with dis?

Apology accepted and I still love you. So much so that I've put together a cheat sheet to get your readers started in this work. I owe a large debt of gratitude to all the women who helped me construct some of these responses, particularly the women of Feminists in Action. CHEAT SHEET ATTACHED!

As your readers continue to engage in this work, I hope they take time to reflect, reassess, and recommit.

Chardi kala.
N

YOUR CHEAT SHEET TO INTERRUPTING SEXIST BULLSHIT

They Say: She has young kids and she's running for office? Who will take care of the kids?

YOU SAY:

- I imagine her partner, if she has one, or a childcare professional, which is probably true of all other candidates with children.
- Who do you think will?
- By running for office and supporting her community, that's how she's taking care of her children.

They Say: She never had children? Or got married? Doesn't that seem kind of weird?

YOU SAY:

- Actually, that's not weird—many women throughout history have not had children. We just don't have that narrative in our everyday lives. And not every woman can have children, nor does every woman want them.
- If she has kids, then the question is who will care for her children, and if she doesn't have children, the question is why doesn't she! I feel like women are caught in a catch-22.

They Say: I'm not going to vote for someone just because she is a woman.

YOU SAY:

- Really? I'm actually going to vote for her because she is a woman. Research has shown that women get more done when in office and get more money for their districts.
- Why not?
- She is not running as a woman, she is running as a candidate.

They Say: I feel like she's playing the race card. Why does she have to remind us that she's a black/brown/Asian woman all the time?

YOU SAY:

- Tell me more—what do you mean?
- She keeps reminding us of her race because the world always reminds her.
- It's not her card, it's her story.

They Say: "Her voice annoys me" or "Her voice is grating. I just don't like listening to her."

YOU SAY:

- Generally speaking, many people have shown they have issues with women's voices. Research has shown that we prefer male voices. For me this suggests that there's a larger issue of unconscious bias at play.

- Isn't it strange that when women raise their voices they are seen as shrill, and when men raise their voices, they are seen as powerful and passionate?
- What voices are you used to listening to?

They Say: She should smile more.

> *YOU SAY:*
> - Why?
> - Do you ever think men should smile more?
> - I didn't realize she was competing for Miss America.

They Say: "She seems angry all the time" or "She's so intense."

> *YOU SAY:*
> - Hmmm . . . I see that as passionate. It seems like she really cares about the issues and representing her constituents.
> - I feel that she has reasonable expectations and is frustrated when they are not met.
> - What do you mean? Can you tell me more?

They Say: She should wait her turn. There are other guys in line for this seat.

> *YOU SAY:*
> - Women have been waiting to have their turn for a long time, don't you think?
> - THERE ARE NO TURNS.
> - It's not the line for the bathroom. That's not how democracy works.

They Say: She's not a viable candidate because she is not raising enough money.

> *YOU SAY:*
> - How much can you give so that she is a viable candidate?
> - It seems like a catch-22. Because she's not raising enough money, she's not seen as a viable candidate. And because she's not seen as a viable candidate, she's not raising enough money!

As Neelamjit reminds us: interrupting sexist and racist conversations, whether they are with others or within ourselves, takes continued work. Our hope is that this cheat sheet is your reminder to do that work. And as you continue to engage in this work, take time to reflect, reassess, and recommit. To help you do that, we've included a brief reading list from Neelamjit on page 230. This list is by no means exhaustive, but it's a good start.

A woman running for office will need people to support her in any way they can. Don't wait to be invited—just start showing up. It's not optional. It's our responsibility.

I'm Running for Office.

THE FINAL CHECKLIST

1. I know why it's IMPERATIVE that more women run for office. ❏

2. I was nominated by _____.

3. Oh, hell yes, I'm qualified to run for office. ❏

4. I'm running for office to _____.

5. The office I'm running for is _____.

6. The filing deadlines for this office are _____.

7. The other requirements for this office are _____.

8. I have met those requirements. ❏

9. I've told these lucky people I'm going to run for office, because making this promise to myself and others matters: _____.

10. I've completed my week of self-promotion. ❏

11. I've built my Campaign Supporter List in a good ol'-fashioned spreadsheet. ❏

12. My fundraising goal is $_____.

13. I've done a full inventory of my online presence and set my damn privacy settings.

14. When asked about any items found online about me (photos, arrests, etc.), I'm going to respond by saying: _____.

15. I absolutely know what I'm going to wear as a candidate. ❏

16. I've found the time to run for office. ❏

17. I've stared at the numbers and have figured out my finances to run for office. ❏

18. I understand how a run will impact my career. ❏

19. I have inventoried my self-care and caregiving, and I know how each will be sacrificed or safeguarded in my run. ❏

20. The incredible organizations I've contacted for help are _____
_____.

21. **These are the women in my life I'm going to ask to run and buy this book for:**

    WOMAN #1. _____   **WOMAN #4.** _____

    WOMAN #2. _____   **WOMAN #5.** _____

    WOMAN #3. _____

She Believed She Could,
SO SHE DID

Hillary Clinton

When we think of Hillary Clinton, the word "first" comes to mind. She was the first First Lady elected to the United States Senate. She was the first woman elected statewide to a federal post from New York State. She was the first woman to earn a major party's nomination for president of the United States and the majority of Americans (65 million, to be exact) voted for her to hold that office. She's held a lot of roles—in addition to the above, she's been the First Lady of Arkansas and the US Secretary of State. She's a mom, a wife, a lawyer, an activist, an author, a grandmother, a leader, and a friend.

In October 2017, she wrote about why more women should run for office. When she wrote these words, Dear Reader, know she was speaking directly to you:

The day after Election Day, I said that women and girls are "valuable and powerful and deserving of every chance and opportunity in the world." I believe in that message more fiercely than ever.

You are valuable and powerful. You are eminently qualified and capable. And I cannot wait to see how you use your unique gifts and skills to make your community, our country, and our world a better place. You can do this. —HILLARY

Goodbye from
JUNE AND KATE

Dear Reader,

We have reached the end. This is going to be harder on us than it is on you. Trust us! Is it okay to say we love you? Fuck it. WE DO LOVE YOU! We love you as much as we love the Monikas and Shawntas and Hildas and Heathers and Beths of the world. Are you wondering if Monika won? If Hilda was able to successfully explain her commitment to her mothering to voters? Did Heather raise enough money? Did Shawnta win? Did Beth? What happened to them?!

Here's the simple truth: some of them won and some of them lost. Some didn't make it past their primary elections. Some of them lost, ran again, and won. And some of them ran, lost, and ran again and lost, but had their lives open up in incredible ways because of their campaigns for public office. Beth, Heather, Shawnta, Monika, and Hilda have stories with a multitude of outcomes. But yours is just beginning.

You just completed a book on running for office. You're the goddamn best. Seriously.

There's one more box to check off.

It's time to cast the first vote for yourself. Go on, write your name. And check that box.

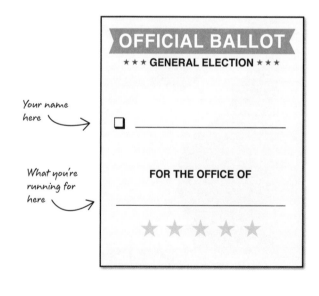

Your name here →

What you're running for here →

This ballot commits you to this goal. Casting a vote for yourself states that you are qualified, that you are worth it, and that you are ready to take the next step.

Now, we have another request. Take a picture of this ballot (we know your phone is right next to you) and share it on your social media platforms. Tag the photo using #REPRESENT. You are joining the ranks of the amazing women before you who have opened up doors for all of us. You are tipping the scale. You are making the world a better place for our children.

You are doing one of the bravest things a woman can do.

And you are not alone.

Use your checklist, engage your networks, call organizations who want to help you win, and then ask for help.

REMINDER: MEN ARE NOT WAITING.

MEN ARE NOT WAITING.

MEN ARE NOT WAITING.

It's time.

At the end of each chapter, we've said, "Keep reading. Stay working. We need you."

But now . . .

Keep running. Start winning. We thank you.

June and *Kate*

DO NOT SKIP THIS

Neelamjit Dhaliwal, who provided the cheat sheet on sexist oppressive language, offers the following reading list to further your understanding of systemic oppression and power.

★ **The New Jim Crow by Michelle Alexander** is a historical account of mass incarceration and how it has disproportionately targeted black men and created a caste-like system in its wake.

★ **Blindspot by Mahzarin Banaji and Anthony Greenwald** helps readers understand that we are all impacted by implicit biases that operate without our consent.

★ **Whistling Vivaldi by Claude Steele** illuminates the powerful effects of stereotypes on our lives.

★ **Yellow by Frank Wu** looks at race beyond black and white with a particular focus on the Asian American experience.

★ **Sister Outsider by Audre Lorde** is a collection of writings by the black lesbian poet and feminist author.

★ **Redefining Realness** introduces readers to **Janet Mock**'s experience of being a trans woman of color.

★ **The Other Slavery by Andrés Reséndez** illuminates the untold story of indigenous enslavement in America.

★ **What Does It Mean to Be White? Developing White Racial Literacy by Robin DiAngelo** helps readers, particularly white readers, better understand their racial identity and the barriers to it.

★ **Stamped from the Beginning by Ibram X. Kendi** chronicles the history of anti-black racism and its primacy in American history, past, present, and future.

★ **Evicted: Poverty and Profit in the American City by Matthew Desmond** follows eight families in Milwaukee as they struggle to maintain their housing, and in doing so, challenges our understanding of poverty and economic exploitation.

★ **Borderlands/La Frontera by Gloria E. Anzaldúa**, a Chicana lesbian, is a semi-autobiographical exploration of how we think about identity through prose and poetry.

★ **We Too Sing America: South Asian, Arab, Muslim, and Sikh Immigrants Shape Our Multiracial Future by Deepa Iyer** chronicles the experiences of South Asian, Arab, Muslim, and Sikh immigrants in America, particularly since 9/11.

DO NOT SKIP THIS EITHER

Were you a little stumped or confused by the white privilege conversation in the introduction? Or maybe you were not sure what we meant by "oppressive language" or wondered just what we were talking about when we asked white women to look at how we have been a part of an unbalanced, unfair, and unjust racial patriarchy? If so, then this essay and its series of twenty-six statements is for you. Take a seat and read about how to unpack the privilege that you walk around with every day. Recognizing and acknowledging it is the best place to start so that you can then do something about it.

White Privilege: Unpacking the Invisible Knapsack
by Peggy McIntosh

Through work to bring materials from Women's Studies into the rest of the curriculum, I have often noticed men's unwillingness to grant that they are over-privileged, even though they may grant that women are disadvantaged. They may say they will work to improve women's status, in the society, the university, or the curriculum, but they can't or won't support the idea of lessening men's. Denials which amount to taboos surround the subject of advantages which men gain from women's disadvantages. These denials protect male privilege from being fully acknowledged, lessened or ended.

Thinking through unacknowledged male privilege as a phenomenon, I realized that, since hierarchies in our society are interlocking, there was most likely a phenomenon of white privilege that was similarly denied and protected. As a white person, I realized I had been taught about racism as something that puts others at a disadvantage, but had been taught not to see one of its corollary aspects, white privilege, which puts me at an advantage.

I think whites are carefully taught not to recognize white privilege, as males are taught not to recognize male privilege. So I have begun in an untutored way to ask what it is like to have white privilege. I have come to see white privilege as an invisible package of unearned assets that I can count on cashing in each day, but about which I was "meant" to remain oblivious. White privilege is like an invisible weightless knapsack of special provisions, maps, passports, codebooks, visas, clothes, tools and blank checks.

Describing white privilege makes one newly accountable. As we in Women's Studies work to reveal male privilege and ask men to give up some of their power, so one who writes about white privilege must ask, "Having described it, what will I do to lessen or end it?"

After I realized the extent to which men work from a base of unacknowledged privilege, I understood that much of their oppressiveness was unconscious. Then I remembered the frequent charges from women of color that white women whom they encounter are oppressive.

I began to understand why we are justly seen as oppressive, even when we don't see ourselves that way. I began to count the ways in which I enjoy unearned skin privilege and have been conditioned into oblivion about its existence.

I was taught to see racism only in individual acts of meanness, not in invisible systems conferring dominance on my group.

My schooling gave me no training in seeing myself as an oppressor, as an unfairly advantaged person, or as a participant in a damaged culture. I was taught to see myself as an individual whose moral state depended on her individual moral will. My schooling followed the pattern my colleague Elizabeth Minnich has pointed out: whites are taught to think of their lives as morally neutral, normative, and average, and also ideal, so that when we work to benefit others, this is seen as work which will allow "them" to be more like "us."

I decided to try to work on myself at least by identifying some of the daily effects of white privilege in my life. I have chosen those conditions which I think in my case attach somewhat more to skin-color privilege than to class, religion, ethnic status, or geographic location, though of course all these other factors are intricately intertwined. As far as I can see, my African American coworkers, friends, and acquaintances with whom I come into daily or frequent contact in this particular time, place and line of work cannot count on most of these conditions.

1. I can if I wish arrange to be in the company of people of my race most of the time.

2. If I should need to move, I can be pretty sure of renting or purchasing housing in an area which I can afford and in which I would want to live.

3. I can be pretty sure that my neighbors in such a location will be neutral or pleasant to me.

4. I can go shopping alone most of the time, pretty well assured that I will not be followed or harassed.

5. I can turn on the television or open to the front page of the paper and see people of my race widely represented.

6. When I am told about our national heritage or about "civilization," I am shown that people of my color made it what it is.

7. I can be sure that my children will be given curricular materials that testify to the existence of their race.

8. If I want to, I can be pretty sure of finding a publisher for this piece on white privilege.

9. I can go into a music shop and count on finding the music of my race represented, into a supermarket and find the staple foods that fit with my cultural traditions, into a hairdresser's shop and find someone who can cut my hair.

10. Whether I use checks, credit cards or cash, I can count on my skin color not to work against the appearance of financial reliability.

11. I can arrange to protect my children most of the time from people who might not like them.

12. I can swear, or dress in secondhand clothes, or not answer letters, without having people attribute these choices to the bad morals, the poverty or the illiteracy of my race.

13. I can speak in public to a powerful male group without putting my race on trial.

14. I can do well in a challenging situation without being called a credit to my race.

15. I am never asked to speak for all the people of my racial group.

16. I can remain oblivious of the language and customs of persons of color who constitute the world's majority without feeling in my culture any penalty for such oblivion.

17. I can criticize our government and talk about how much I fear its policies and behavior without being seen as a cultural outsider.

18. I can be pretty sure that if I ask to talk to "the person in charge," I will be facing a person of my race.

19. If a traffic cop pulls me over or if the IRS audits my tax return, I can be sure I haven't been singled out because of my race.

20. I can easily buy posters, postcards, picture books, greeting cards, dolls, toys and children's magazines featuring people of my race.

21. I can go home from most meetings of organizations I belong to feeling somewhat tied in, rather than isolated, out-of-place, outnumbered, unheard, held at a distance or feared.

22. I can take a job with an affirmative action employer without having co-workers on the job suspect that I got it because of race.

23. I can choose public accommodations without fearing that people of my race cannot get in or will be mistreated in the places I have chosen.

24. I can be sure that if I need legal or medical help, my race will not work against me.

25. If my day, week, or year is going badly, I need not ask of each negative episode or situation whether it has racial overtones.

26. I can choose blemish cover or bandages in "flesh" color and have them more or less match my skin.

I repeatedly forgot each of the realizations on this list until I wrote it down. For me, white privilege has turned out to be an elusive and fugitive subject. The pressure to avoid it is great, for in facing it I must give up the myth of meritocracy. If these things are true, this is not such a free country; one's life is not what one makes it; many doors open for certain people through no virtues of their own.

In unpacking this invisible knapsack of white privilege, I have listed conditions of daily experience that I once took for granted. Nor did I think of any of these perquisites as bad for the holder. I now think that we need a more finely differentiated taxonomy of privilege, for some of these varieties are only what one would want for everyone in a just society, and others give license to be ignorant, oblivious, arrogant and destructive.

I see a pattern running through the matrix of white privilege, a pattern of assumptions that were passed on to me as a white person. There was one main piece of cultural turf; it was my own turf, and I was among those who could control the turf. My skin color was an asset for any move I was educated to want to make. I could think of myself as belonging in major ways and of making social systems work for me. I could freely disparage, fear, neglect or be oblivious to anything outside of the dominant cultural forms. Being of the main culture, I could also criticize it fairly freely.

In proportion as my racial group was being made confident, comfortable and oblivious, other groups were likely being made inconfident, uncomfortable and alienated. Whiteness protected me from many kinds of hostility, distress and violence, which I was being subtly trained to visit, in turn, upon people of color.

For this reason, the word "privilege" now seems to me misleading. We usually think of privilege as being a favored state, whether earned or conferred by birth or luck. Yet some of the conditions I have described here work systematically to overempower certain groups. Such privilege simply confers dominance because of one's race or sex.

I want, then, to distinguish between earned strength and unearned power conferred systemically. Power from unearned privilege can look like strength when it is in fact permission to escape or to dominate. But not all of the privileges on my list are inevitably damaging. Some, like the expectation that neighbors will be decent to you, or that your race will not count against you in court, should be the norm in a just society. Others, like the privilege to ignore less powerful people, distort the humanity of the holders as well as the ignored groups.

We might at least start by distinguishing between positive advantages, which we can work to spread, and negative types of advantage, which unless rejected will always reinforce our present hierarchies. For example, the feeling that one belongs within the human circle, as Native Americans say, should not be seen as privilege for a few. Ideally it is an unearned entitlement. At present, since only a few have it, it is an unearned advantage for them. This paper results from a process of coming to see that some of the power that I originally saw as attendant on being a human being in the United States consisted in unearned advantage and conferred dominance.

The question is: "Having described white privilege, what will I do to end it?"

I have met very few men who are truly distressed about systemic, unearned male advantage and conferred dominance. And so one question for me and others like me is whether we will be like them, or whether we will get truly distressed, even outraged, about unearned race advantage and conferred dominance, and, if so, what will we do to lessen them. In any case, we need to do more work in identifying how they actually affect our daily lives. Many, perhaps most, of our white students in the US think that racism doesn't affect them because they are not people of color, they do not see "whiteness" as a racial identity. In addition, since race and sex are not the only advantaging systems at work, we need similarly to examine the daily experience of having age advantage, or ethnic advantage, or physical ability, or advantage related to nationality, religion or sexual orientation.

Difficulties and dangers surrounding the task of finding parallels are many. Since racism, sexism and heterosexism are not the same, the advantages associated with them should not be seen as the same. In addition, it is hard to disentangle aspects of unearned advantage which rest more on social class, economic class, race, religion, sex and ethnic identity than on other factors. Still, all of the oppressions are interlocking, as the Combahee River Collective Statement of 1977 continues to remind us eloquently.

One factor seems clear about all of the interlocking oppressions. They take both active forms, which we can see, and embedded forms, which as a member of the dominant group one is taught not to see. In my class and place, I did not see myself as a racist because I was taught to recognize racism only in individual acts of meanness by members of my group, never in invisible systems conferring unsought racial dominance on my group from birth.

Disapproving of the systems won't be enough to change them. I was taught to think that racism could end if white individuals changed their attitudes. But a "white" skin in the United States opens many doors for whites whether or not we approve of the way dominance has been conferred on us. Individual acts can palliate, but cannot end, these problems.

To redesign social systems, we need first to acknowledge their colossal unseen dimensions. The silences and denials surrounding privilege are the key political tool here. They keep the thinking about equality or equity incomplete, protecting unearned advantage and conferred dominance by making these taboo subjects. Most talk by whites about equal opportunity seems to me now to be about equal opportunity to try to get into a position of dominance while denying that systems of dominance exist.

It seems to me that obliviousness about white advantage, like obliviousness about male advantage, is kept strongly inculturated in the United States so as to maintain the myth of meritocracy, the myth that democratic choice is equally available to all. Keeping most people unaware that freedom of confident action is there for just a small number of people props up those in power and serves to keep power in the hands of the same groups that have most of it already.

Although systemic change takes many decades, there are pressing questions for me and I imagine for some others like me if we raise our daily consciousness on the perquisites of being lightskinned. What will we do with such knowledge? As we know from watching men, it is an open question whether we will choose to use unearned advantage to weaken hidden systems of advantage, and whether we will use any of our arbitrarily awarded power to try to reconstruct power systems on a broader base.

This is an authorized excerpt of McIntosh's original white privilege article, "White Privilege and Male Privilege: A Personal Account of Coming to See Correspondences through Work in Women's Studies," Working Paper 189 (1988), Wellesley Centers for Women, Wellesley College, MA, 02481.

"White Privilege: Unpacking the Invisible Knapsack" first appeared in *Peace and Freedom* magazine, July/August, 1989, pp. 10-12, a publication of the Women's International League for Peace and Freedom, Philadelphia, PA.

Anyone who wishes to reproduce more than 35 copies of this article must apply to the author, Dr. Peggy McIntosh, at mmcintosh@wellesley.edu. This article may not be electronically posted except by the National SEED Project.

ACKNOWLEDGMENTS
and a few more dedications

There are a few brave souls who fought to be our first, Dear Readers. To the people who read our proposal—even the very early drafts—thank you! To Kulap Vilaysack, Casey Wilson, Sarah Locke, Morgan Walsh, Matt McConkey, and Deanna and Wing Cheng, thank you for taking the time to provide your thoughts and feedback. To Matt Burgess, Jen O'Malley Dillon, and Jessica Post, thank you for reading that very long first draft and for your suggestions. To Neelamjit Dhaliwal, Samara Bay, and Jera Mehrdad, thank you for your expertise and insight. To The Jane Club, FIA, and Jon Stern, thank you for providing space to meet, discuss, and work on this project. Ellen Malcolm, Stephanie Schriock, Emily Cain, Jess O'Connell, thank you for your incredible support and all that you do to help women run and win. We would also like to thank the Center for Women in American Politics at Rutgers for their very helpful resources and research on women candidates.

> For my parents, thank you for teaching me about engagement and responsibility. I hope this book helps create a world that is better than the one you left. For Gus and Sam Scheer, I hope this book helps create a world that you deserve. Thank you for being a constant source of inspiration and motivation and for being so damn cute. For Paul, thank you for your first read and immediate phone call and for making all of my dreams come true. I'm but a shell without you.

JUNE

Thank you to David Kuhn and Kate Mack at Aevitas for believing in this book from our very first call. Thank you to our editor, Margot Herrera, at Workman, for her thoughtful questions and endless enthusiasm and encouragement. Thanks also to the team that works with her: art director Becky Terhune, production editor Kim Daly, typesetter extraordinaire Barbara Peragine, and publicity and marketing mavens Chloe Puton, Rebecca Carlisle, and Moira Kerrigan.

KATE

To my husband, Sam, thank you for encouraging me to start this creative journey. I couldn't have done this without your love and support. To my son Charlie, I hope I make you proud. To my parents, brother, extended family, and friends: thank you for your feedback and your inspiration, your encouragement and love. This book would not be where it is today without all of you.

Thank you to the women candidates and leaders who agreed to share their wisdom, insights, and lessons with us and our readers. To Congresswoman Pramila Jayapal, Congresswoman Ayanna Pressley, former Colorado Speaker Crisanta Duran, Mayor Jenny Durkan, City Councilwoman Liz Brown, and Library Trustee and Town Constable Jordan Evans—thank you for being so generous with your time and for being open to this project.

This book is dedicated to the women leaders who came before us, the women leaders who are currently fighting for us, and the women leaders who will come after us. Thank you.